MARINE ENGINEER[

GW00788615

Volume 1

Part 5

FIRE FIGHTING EQUIPMENT
AND ITS USE IN SHIPS

by

G. VICTORY, C.Eng., F.I.Mar.E.

and

I. H. OWEN, C.Eng., M.I.Mar.E.

THE INSTITUTE OF MARINE ENGINEERS

Published for The Institute of Marine Engineers

by

Marine Management (Holdings) Ltd.

76 Mark Lane, London EC3R 7JN

(England Reg. No. 1100685)

First Reprint January 1979
Second Reprint April 1981

ISBN: 0 900976 14 4

LCCCN: 74–76226

Printed in England by The Chameleon Press Ltd. London

CONTENTS

ACKNOWLEDGEMENTS

The authors gratefully acknowledge the following companies as the sources of illustrations used in this Part:

Angus Fire Armour (a Division of George Angus & Co. Ltd.)
BP Tanker Company Ltd.
British Standards Institution
Chubb Fire Security Ltd.
de boer n.v., Netherlands
Distillers Company (Carbon Dioxide) Ltd.
Ginge Fire and Electronics Ltd., Denmark
L & G Fire Appliance Co. Ltd.
Lux Brandslukning A/S, Norway

Mather and Platt Ltd.
Minerva Fire Defence (EMI) Ltd.
nu-swift International Ltd.
Rampart Engineering Co. Ltd.
Royal Institution of Naval Architects
Salen and Wicander, Sweden
Seetru Ltd.
Siebe Gorman and Co. Ltd.
Skuteng A/S, Norway
Svenska Skumslacknings AB, Sweden
The Walter Kidde Co. Ltd.

INTRODUCTION

The scope of this subject is so vast that only a condensed version can be given in the space available.

This resumé is principally intended for the Junior Engineer going to sea and studying for his Certificates, but it may be used with advantage as a work of reference by certificated engineers in search of information on modern equipment.

Numerous books and pamphlets are referred to in the Bibliography for those who wish to extend their knowledge of the subject.

Fire at sea can be ugly and terrifying to those unfortunate enough to experience it. A ship would be a poor fire risk by any standard with its combination of living quarters, cargo spaces, fuel tanks and machinery in such a confined space; when, in addition, in the event of a fire, it is neither possible to summon outside aid in the form of a Fire Brigade, nor retreat from it without taking to the boats, the full dangers of a shipboard fire are more clearly seen.

If a fire should break out on a ship how best can it be dealt with?

Firstly, by adopting the right mental attitude. Fire should not be thought of as an inanimate object. A fire which starts unseen as a small flicker of flame may grow at such a pace that it can quickly get out of hand. Once found it must be extinguished with all the speed and means available or it will destroy those who seek to restrain it. Fire, when apparently extinguished, can spring to life should some untrained person assume that because the flames have gone the danger is passed.

Secondly, by considering each fire as an individual occurrence. The correct action in each case will depend on the position of the fire, the combustibles involved, and the combustibles which are in danger of becoming involved. There is no hard and fast rule, and the correct action can only be assessed by one who has knowledge and training.

Thirdly, by ensuring that properly maintained appliances are available for personnel to use, and that all fire fighting, fire detecting and fire alarm systems are in fully operational order. Marine Engineers may go to sea trained as craftsmen in the use of tools, they may go to sea knowing how a marine power plant operates, but the only fire they are likely to have met with is the one in the hearth at home. Yet, once at sea, they may have to assume the specialized role of fire fighter at any time, so they must quickly learn all they can about the prevention and extinction of fire. With knowledge and ability they can attack a fire in the right manner and, by knowing its weaknesses, extinguish it in a short time. Without knowledge and ability, the fire will find out their weaknesses, for fire is a foe against which no liberties can be taken.

1. HISTORICAL

From early times up to the 19th Century, the design of ships, their safety and that of the cargo and crew were matters entirely in the hands of the owners. Admittedly, Trinity House, that ancient guild of pilots and mariners, during the 16th and 17th Centuries had supervized the building of ships to some extent; but its authority had waned by the end of the latter period and for the next century and a half there was no authority to take its place.

With the volume of trade growing and with increased emigration, the demand for bigger and faster ships grew and it was not surprising that in this race, cargo carrying capacity took precedence over the safety of both ship and crew.

By the early 19th Century, British shipping was in a desperate state, the number of ships and men being lost reaching unprecedented proportions. The Navigation Laws, under whose protectionist policy the British merchant fleet had operated, were also repealed in 1849 and it was becoming obvious that Government intervention in some form was necessary if the country was to retain its position as one of the great seafaring nations.

It was against this background that the Mercantile Marine Act of 1850 was introduced which established a Marine Department at the Board of Trade. In the following year, the Steam Navigation Act of 1851 was enacted, this marking the beginning of Government involvement in the safety and seaworthiness of ships. The monumental Shipping Act of 1894, still on the statute book and known in shipping circles as the Principal Act, was a milestone in maritime legislation and from it all present legislation stems. In 1949 the Safety Convention Act gave the Government powers to prepare rules in respect of, *inter alia*, fire appliances and resulted in the promulgation of the Merchant Shipping (Fire Appliances) Rules 1952. As a result of the international conference on Safety of Life at Sea held under the auspices of the Intergovernmental Maritime Consultative Organization in 1960, usually referred to as IMCO, these rules were superseded in due course by the Merchant Shipping (Fire Appliances) Rules 1965. These last named rules detail the arrangements and equipment necessary for fire detection, prevention and extinction, which must, by law, be provided on British ships today; any ambitious marine engineer is advised to be aware of their existence, if not of their detailed contents.

3

2. THE CHARACTER OF FIRE

Fire is an external sign of chemical action, usually the combination of carbon and hydrogen with oxygen, resulting in the release of heat energy. Only gas can be ignited. To start the action it is necessary either to apply a flame or a spark having a certain minimum energy value to a substance which has been raised to a temperature sufficient to release flammable vapours conducive to the continuation of the action; or else to raise the substance to its auto-ignition temperature or temperature, where spontaneous combustion of the liberated gases occurs. Once started, the heat energy released is available to raise a greater amount of the substance to the temperature of combustion, so the amount of gases liberated and of burning material increases and the fire spreads ever more rapidly. If the temperature is near that of self-ignition, little energy is required to cause combustion, and fires will appear to break out at points some distance from the main fire at a bewildering speed. Given a good start and plenty of combustible material, most fires are eventually limited only by the rate at which air can get to the burning material. There are limits to the air/fuel ratio at which different substances will burn, and limitation of air will cause long tongues of flame to reach out searching for the air required. Incomplete combustion can result in the formation of pockets of gas which may explode if sufficient air becomes available, whilst heated hydrocarbons, if lacking air, will decompose and form the sooty and tarry particles characteristic of thick, black smoke.

There are three requirements covering the propagation of practically all fires:

1) a combustible material;
2) a supply of oxygen usually in the form of air;
3) a source of heat or ignition.

Similarly, there are three basic ways of fighting a fire:

1) by removing the combustible material;
2) by preventing the supply of oxygen;
3) by using a cooling medium to reduce the temperature of the material to a point where combustion ceases.

Most successful fire fighting techniques use a combination of two or all of these methods, though any one will subdue a fire.

The combustible materials commonly found on ships fall into two groups:

a) solid materials such as wood, paper, coal and cloth;
b) liquid materials, mainly fuel and lubricating oil.

For fires involving solid materials, water jet cooling or inert gas smothering are usually applied with the emphasis on cooling, whilst for fires involving liquid fuels cooling by water spray and smothering by either inert gas or a foam blanket are all possibilities.

The techniques in fighting fires involving explosives and the multiplicity of dangerous goods and chemicals now being transported by sea in bulk as well as in packages, is too specialized a subject to be dealt with here.*

---

* Further information may be found in the publication "Recommended Code for the Construction and Equipment of Ships Carrying Dangerous Liquid Chemicals in Bulk", issued by the Marine Division of the Department of Trade and Industry and in the "Carriage of Dangerous Goods in Ships", second edition 1971, as amended September 1972, issued by H.M. Stationery Office.

3. PRECAUTION AGAINST FIRE

The only sure way to avoid the consequence of a disastrous fire at sea is not to have one. Most ship fires in peace time are caused by carelessness, ignorance, or stupidity. It is therefore the duty of all seafarers to see that they are not found guilty on any of these counts.

In accommodation the greatest attention must be paid to the safe disposal of cigarette ends and matches. One should always be certain that the match is actually extinguished and the cigarette end properly stubbed out before being put in a safe receptacle. The rotating top type of ash tray is safest as there is no chance of the contents being scattered around the cabin should the ash-tray slide off the table in rough weather. Matches should not be kept loose and should be safety type, though this name should not be taken too literally as they are still liable to self-ignition under certain circumstances. All electrical appliances must be firmly secured and served by permanent connexions wherever possible. If flexible leads must be used they should be as short as possible and so arranged that chafing or cutting of the wires in service is not possible, whilst the correct size of plug and socket with an effective earth connexion should be used. Cases have been found where two loose wires to a portable lamp were merely held into a socket by matchsticks, and fires have been caused by portable lamps being so placed that they fell over in rough weather. Heat from the electric light bulb itself can ignite combustible material and this is an all too common cause of fire. Makeshift paper shades, deeply charred, have been found in cabins and the occupants seem to have been blissfully unaware of the danger. On no account should combustible material be allowed to come into contact with a naked light bulb—proper shades should be provided. The correctly rated fuse should always be used in a circuit. When a fuse burns out repeatedly, one of heavier load is often fitted though the fault, which may be in the wiring, remains undetected. Similarly, the addition of extra appliances to a circuit which is not designed to carry the additional load will cause the wires to overheat, producing failure of the insulation, a short circuit and the resultant fire.

The most usual cause of accommodation fires, however, has been the habit of smoking in bed. It seems beyond comprehension that people do not realize that just before sleeping the senses are dulled and it is impossible to be certain that the last cigarette will be properly extinguished. Although people know that this action has cost the lives of many others, they still believe that they could not make such a mistake as to fall asleep whilst smoking.

Many fires have originated in ships' galleys, generally because of over-heated pans of fat catching fire, but sometimes because of oil leakage where oil fired cooking stoves were fitted.

In cargo spaces, proper stowage and ventilation should prevent over-heating and possible spontaneous combustion and, providing no cigarette ends or unextinguished matches are dropped among the cargo, it will be safe. Illegal smoking in cargo and storage compartments and in forbidden spaces such as the centre-castle on tankers has taken a heavy toll of both ships and crews.

In the machinery spaces, precautions should mainly take the form of cleanliness, the prevention of oil leakage, and the removal of all combustible materials from vulnerable positions. Even a thick accumulation of paint, often found in old ships, can help to spread a fire. To prevent oil escaping unseen the pipes carrying hot oil under pressure should be above the floor plates, lighting above and below the floor plates should be bright and comprehensive, and clean save-alls should be placed under the burners and filters. Oil burners should be carefully assembled and any which drip oil or burn unevenly should be changed. Care should be taken before changing burners and filters to ensure that there is no pressure on them when they are opened. All joints and glands in oil lines and at pumps should be kept tight and leakage prevented, whilst all boundary bars and the oil tight coamings designed to contain any overflow of oil should be intact and kept clean. Oil should not be allowed to accumulate on tank tops or in bilges and special care must be taken to prevent any uncontrollable overflow of oil from storage or settling tanks. In this respect, some of the arrangements provided in older ships for overflow pipes and for gauging the contents of the settling tanks were very dangerous. With the older float and wire type of gauge, which fortunately is rarely found nowadays, the pulley carrying the wire was often not carried far enough above the top of the tank, so that should the tank be overfilled the oil could overflow into the engine room or over the boilers. Fires are still caused by overflow pipes not being led to a safe place and by loose or missing flange covers on the top of the tank. Oil level indicators should be of a type which will not allow oil to escape in the event of damage to them and it is preferable that they should be of a type which does not require piercing of the lower part of the tank. Wood, paints, spirits, tins of oil and rags or waste should not be kept in boiler rooms or machinery spaces, secure stowage in the tunnel or steering gear flat being suitable for such items, whilst dirty oil and oily rags should not be allowed to accumulate. All electric wiring should be permanent, well maintained and kept clean and dry, and not overloaded by the gradual addition of extra appliances.

The question of smoking in the machinery spaces is a vexed one. It seems evident however that even in places where the danger is greater than in ship's engine and boiler rooms, it is impossible to make certain that a no smoking rule can be enforced, so that it is better to admit that people will smoke, and to provide suitable receptacles for the disposal of the cigarette stubs. Certain ships, e.g. tankers and certain bulk dangerous goods carriers, will of course have to restrict the places where smoking may be allowed, but it seems wise to ensure that any person wishing to smoke should have the opportunity of doing so in a safe place at reasonable intervals.

4. FIRE EXTINGUISHING APPLIANCES

4.1. WATER PUMPS, HYDRANTS AND HOSES

The finest cooling medium and the most universal fire extinguisher of all is water. For carbonaceous materials, which are usually absorbent, a copious supply is preferred, whilst for hydrocarbon materials, which in ships are usually oils, the water should be broken into small particles in a special nozzle to give the greatest heat absorbing surface area and to prevent any disturbance of the surface of the burning liquid. Water, even in the form of a spray, is of little use on spirit or petrol fires and it is safer not to use it on electrical appliances as it will act as a conductor (particularly if sea water) and can result in the operator receiving a severe shock.

Imagine how happy a fire brigade would be if they were called to a fire which was entirely surrounded by water. Their greatest worry regarding adequate supplies would be non-existent, and they would be able to get on with the job without having to run out and couple up long lengths of hose. Yet this is the position aboard ship, and if we can only ensure that this water will be readily available at a suitable pressure with the hoses and nozzles appropriate to the type of fire, we will be well equipped to deal with almost any eventuality.

Most ships have an arrangement of fire main and hydrant valves whereby at least two jets of water may be directed on a fire in any part of the ship. The water supply to the fire main is generally provided by at least two power operated pumps in the machinery spaces, together with an alternative supply which can be brought into operation should the engine room be untenable. This is usually provided by a separate auxiliary pump driven by a diesel engine or by an electric motor coupled to an emergency generator. A shut-off valve is fitted in the rising main from the engine room and may be operated from outside the space, so that if the engine room is abandoned the emergency pump can supply the deck line even if there is a burst water main in the engine room. The fire main can also be pressurized, if necessary, from the shore or another ship by use of the international shore connexion. The ideal arrangement, particularly in accommodation spaces, should allow one person to run out sufficient hose, preferably from a reel, and by merely opening one valve to have an adequate jet or spray immediately available so that any fire could be dealt with before it could get a good hold. Such an arrangement is shown in Fig. 1.

FIG. 1.—*Hose reel unit.*

If a suitable water pressure of about 3 bars (40 lb/in^2) were immediately available at any hydrant on the ship, and hoses could be permanently fitted so that one person could bring a hose into action immediately, then many serious fires would be extinguished at a very early stage. Why is this happy state of affairs so seldom found in practice?

With the usual system having fixed piping with no reservoir, and allowing for the pressure head from the engine room to the upper deck and the pressure loss in the pipes, it is necessary to maintain about 6 bars (80 lb/in^2) pressure at the pump, and this involves having a pump churning around with little or no delivery for 24 hours a day. Frequent overhauling of the pump is necessary in these conditions and hence it is common practice to slow down the pump, or to stop it altogether, so that when water is required in a hurry there is either an inadequate trickle or none at all. A commonly used alternative was to have the fire main combined with the sanitary system, which requires a lower pressure, so that if water was required for fire fighting purposes the valves to the sanitary tank had to be closed before the pressure could be boosted to give a suitable supply at the fire hydrant; this again was unsatisfactory and is indeed forbidden under the Merchant Shipping (Fire Appliances) Rules 1965. It would seem that the best way to maintain an adequate pressure in the line without having a continuously running pump is to fit a reserve tank, partially water-filled and pressurized with air, combined with a pressure operated water pump which cuts in when the pressure and water level in the tank are reduced and cuts out again when the pressure and water level in the tank rise to the required value. This method is used in the "sprinkler" system to be described later and its more general adoption to the hydrant system would be a great step forward.

Fire hose is usually 63·5 mm (2½ in) diameter canvas in 9 m (30 ft) or 18 m (60 ft) lengths, though other material with plastic or rubber lining is available. It is usually carried in a tight roll, which means that the entire length has to be unrolled before a nozzle can be fitted and it can be coupled to the hydrant and allow water to pass; it is also often very difficult to accommodate it all if the fire is close to the hydrant. In addition, the 63·5 mm (2½ in) hose is rather stiff and therefore difficult to bend around corners without forming a kink which shuts off the water supply. Hoses not coupled to hydrants are preferably rolled double, i.e. from the centre towards the two ends (the Dutch Roll), this being much easier to run out.

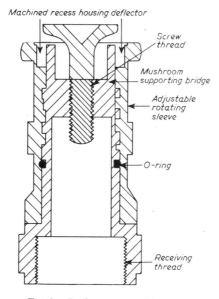

FIG. 2.—*Dual purpose nozzle.*

In the machinery spaces where time is vital, hoses with spray nozzles (Fig. 2) should be permanently attached to hydrants at strategic positions, and ideally should have a supply of water at a suitable pressure available at all times, requiring only that the hose be run out and the valve opened so that an effective spray may quickly be played on any fire that may occur. For this purpose the hose is usually "flaked", that is, stowed in a zig-zag manner similar to the legs of a jumping cracker firework. However, the entire hose has to be laid out before it can be used, so again it would be better if a non-collapsible hose could be carried on a reel having a trunnion supply as recommended for the accommodation.

In both machinery and accommodation spaces, the difficulties of laying out and handling lengths of 63·5 mm ($2\frac{1}{2}$ in) diameter canvas hose are obvious. Experience has shown that generally the throughput of water in a 44·5 mm ($1\frac{3}{4}$ in) diameter lined hose is comparable to that in a 63·5 mm ($2\frac{1}{2}$ in) diameter canvas hose of the same length and at the same pressure and consequently increasing use is being made in these locations of the smaller size hose.

To assist in the extinction of ship fires many special fire appliances have been developed, both as portable and as fixed installations, and these are dealt with below.

4.2 PORTABLE EXTINGUISHERS

4.2.1. Soda–Acid Extinguisher

The simplest extinguisher, in the event of a small fire in a cabin, is a bucket of water. However, it is difficult to deposit the water on the right spot from any distance, and usually it all goes in one throw. So a portable device which would project a jet of water with accuracy over a greater distance and for a longer period of time is required. This has led to the development of the common 9 l (2 gal) soda–acid extinguisher (Fig. 3), which is fitted in the accommodation of most ships. Although the relevant British Standard Specification, i.e. BS 138 : 1948 "Portable Fire Extinguishers of the Water Type (Soda Acid)", permits such extinguishers to be cylindrical or conical in shape, those used on ships are invariably of the former type. The cylindrical sheil, which is about 178 mm (7 in) diameter and 533 mm (21 in) high, and the dished ends, are usually made of 16 or 18 gauge steel although other materials such as copper are allowed. The extinguisher body is coated internally with lead, zinc or tin to prevent corrosion, although plastic linings are being developed and are becoming more popular. The thickness is sufficient to safely withstand the internal pressure which may result if the outlet became choked after the extinguisher had been operated. In accordance with the Standard, this shall not exceed 17 bar (250 lb/in^2) at 21°C (70°F). The dishing is generally outward so as to reduce corrosion at the joints which are invariably welded nowadays, though riveted joints are permitted in which case they must also be soldered. To ensure that the containers are

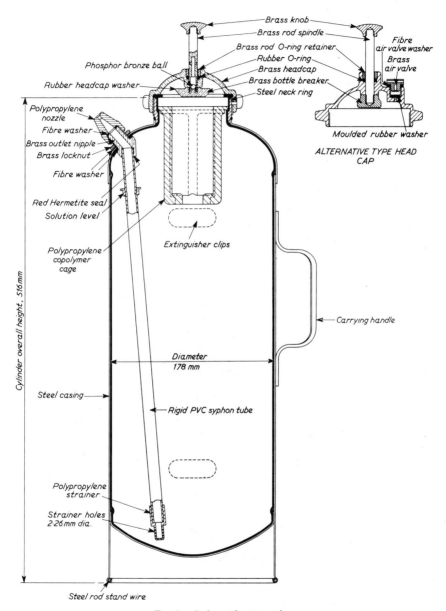

Brass knob
Brass rod spindle
Brass rod O-ring retainer
Fibre air valve washer
Rubber O-ring
Brass headcap
Brass air valve
Phosphor bronze ball
Brass bottle breaker
Rubber headcap washer
Steel neck ring

Polypropylene nozzle
Fibre washer
Brass outlet nipple
Brass locknut
Fibre washer
Red Hermetite seal
Solution level
Polypropylene copolymer cage

Moulded rubber washer

ALTERNATIVE TYPE HEAD CAP

Extinguisher clips

Cylinder overall height, 516 mm

Diameter 178 mm

Carrying handle

Steel casing

Rigid PVC syphon tube

Polypropylene strainer
Strainer holes 2·26 mm dia.

Steel rod stand wire

FIG. 3.—*Soda–acid extinguisher.*

strong enough they are tested hydraulically when new to 24 bars ($350 \, lb/in^2$), the pressure being maintained for 5 min. Subsequent tests are made every 4 years to 21 bars ($300 \, lb/in^2$). In some cases where containers have been tested to destruction they have withstood pressures of over 48 bars ($700 \, lb/in^2$), the barrelling of the body before rupture occurred being very pronounced. The upper convex end of the shell incorporates a steel or copper alloy neck ring, having an internal opening at least 57 mm ($2\frac{1}{4}$ in) diameter to allow for the introduction of the charges and for effective internal inspection, being closed by a screwed stainless steel or copper alloy cap having small holes or slots in the threads so that any internal pressure must be released before the cap can be fully removed. Other features are a filter in the discharge nozzle and a device to prevent the contents of the extinguisher rising in the discharge tube, if one is fitted, due to a rise in temperature of the surrounding atmosphere. It may take the form of a small ball release valve shown in Fig. 3 in the plunger spindle though a disc release valve in the body often serves the same purpose. A clearly marked panel on the outside must give, *inter alia*, the following information:

a) instructions for operating the extinguisher;
b) the capacity of the extinguisher and the level to which it is filled in its working condition;
c) the pressure to which the extinguisher has been tested;
d) the maker and year of manufacture.

In the usual type, the acid charge is contained in a sealed glass vessel, which is broken by the operating spindle being struck, thus permitting the acid to mix with the alkali solution in the outer container and causing the extinguisher to operate. In order to charge the extinguisher, about 454 g (16 oz) of an alkali, sodium bicarbonate, is thoroughly mixed in warm water to make 9 l (2 gal) of solution, which is poured into the outer container and should come up to the level indicator. A small, sealed glass vessel holding 57 g (2 oz) of sulphuric acid is placed in the perforated container in the air space above the liquid, and the cap is screwed down on to the jointing. To operate the extinguisher, the knob on the top is given a sharp blow; this breaks the bottle allowing the acid to mix with the alkaline solution, thus promoting a chemical reaction. The pressure of the CO_2 so formed accumulates in the chamber and ejects the contents, the small pressure relief valve having been closed by the rapid rise in pressure.

The equation for the chemical reaction is as follows:

$$H_2SO_4 \quad + \quad 2NaHCO_3 \quad = \quad Na_2SO_4 \quad + \quad 2H_2O \quad + \quad 2CO_2$$

Sulphuric acid	Sodium bicarbonate	Sodium sulphate	Water	Carbon dioxide

The extinguisher with the sealed acid charge does not require to be turned upside down to operate it, so it has an internal tube. If it should be turned upside down little or no discharge will take place as the gas can escape freely and there will be no build up of pressure. Soda–acid extinguishers are useful on carbonaceous fires, usually in accommodation, involving wood, paper and furnishings, where the primary purpose is to reduce the temperature of the burning material without doing more damage to the surroundings than is necessary. It will project fluid more than 6 m (20 ft) for a period of not less than 1 min through a nozzle the design and area of orifice of which are such that the extinguisher is completely discharged in not more than 2 min.

4.2.2. Chemical Foam Extinguishers*

With oil fires however, such a jet of water is not effective as it disturbs the surface and spreads the oil, so it would be better if we could apply some substance which would cover the surface and prevent the supply of air so necessary to combustion. This is embodied in the typical chemical foam extinguisher (Fig. 4) which has been adapted from the soda–acid extinguisher by adding a foam-making substance to give the liquid a soapy consistency capable of forming bubbles having a tough impervious skin. It is usually found in machinery spaces and other locations where an oil fire may occur. The requirements for the shell are as for the soda–acid extinguisher, the relevant British Standard Specification being BS 740 : Part 1 : 1948 "Portable Fire Extinguishers of the Foam Type (Chemical)", but a larger amount of weaker acid solution is placed in the inner container, which is sealed by a cap. This inner container may be made of copper covered with lead, but brass, porcelain, glass and polythene may also be used. The inner container is filled to the correct level with a solution of aluminium sulphate which acts as weak acid in this case and as this is usually supplied in powder form it must be carefully mixed with the right amount of warm water before being inserted, just as is the powder containing the mixture of sodium bicarbonate and stabilizer which is put in the outer container. When the sealing cap is released by the operating handle and the extinguisher is inverted the liquids mix, carbon dioxide gas is generated, and the pressure ejects the contents just as in the soda–acid type. To assist the action one should place a finger over the nozzle after inverting and shake the extinguisher. The minimum period for which the 6 m (20 ft) jet must be maintained however is 30 sec and the maximum period of complete discharge of the expellable foam is 90 sec. The equation for the chemical reaction in this case is

$$Al_2(SO_4)_3 \quad + \quad 6NaHCO_3 \quad = \quad 2Al(OH)_3 \quad + \quad 3Na_2SO_4 \quad + \quad 6CO_2$$

Aluminium sulphate	Sodium bicarbonate	Aluminium hydroxide	Sodium sulphate	Carbon dioxide

It will be seen that the chemical action is fundamentally the same as in the soda–acid type, the weaker acid being used mainly to slow down the action to prevent too high a pressure being generated, and to give time for the

---

* Official publications often refer to "Froth" extinguishers. These are the same as "Foam" extinguishers, but the latter description is more generally used by commercial extinguisher manufacturers and shore based authorities.

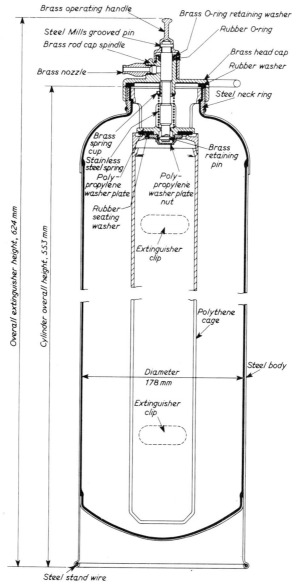

FIG. 4.—*Foam extinguisher (polythene lined).*

bubbles to form. The evolution of the bubbles, which in this case leads to the formation of what is referred to as "Chemical" foam, results from the foam-making substances which are added to the sodium bicarbonate in the outer container. These substances are called stabilizers because they produce a stable foam consisting of a large mass of carbon dioxide bubbles having a strong durable skin. Among the substances used are extracts of liquorice root, or of the bark of the Aquilla tree (sometimes referred to as "Soap bark"), whilst "Turkey-red" oil, saponine, Fuller's earth, and albumin have all been used for this purpose. The ratio of foam produced to liquid varies from 8:1 to 12:1, so that a 9 l (2 gal) extinguisher should produce between 5 and 7 l (16 and 24 gal) of foam. As this extinguisher has to be turned upside down to operate it, it does not have an internal pipe.

These then, are what might be called the "bread and butter" extinguishers, the soda–acid being usually found in the accommodation and the foam type being found in the machinery spaces of ships. They have their faults, in that the action tends to be very slow in cold weather, and hence the jet is poor, whilst the charges particularly in foam extinguishers tend to deteriorate in hot weather, or when located in a hot position, also the soda–acid type can cause damage to furnishings if the acid is not entirely neutralized in the action. This has resulted in the development of other types of portable extinguishers which do not have these disadvantages and these are now in general use.

4.2.3. Extinguishers of the Gas Pressurized Water Type

Figure 5 shows a typical extinguisher of this type but the relevant British Standard specification BS 1382 : 1948 "Portable Fire Extinguishers of the Water Type (Gas Pressure)" does permit the gas container to be fitted internally or externally and for the extinguisher to be used in the upright or inverted position. A move is afoot, however, to standardize the operating position. In the type illustrated, the charge of plain water can be ejected by bursting the sealing disc of the container holding the gas charge, usually about 63 g (2 oz) of liquid CO_2, the extinguisher being used in the upright position. The construction and discharge rate are similar to those of the soda–acid extinguisher.

4.2.4. Extinguishers of the Gas Pressurized Foam Type

Figure 6 depicts a typical extinguisher of this type, the relevant British Standard Specification being BS 740 : Part 2 : 1952 "Portable Fire Extinguishers of the Foam Type (Gas Pressure)". The construction and method of operation of this type of extinguisher are similar to that of the gas pressurized water type but its discharge rate is the same as that for chemical foam extinguishers. In this case there is no chemical action, but the liquid is directed through a hose to a special nozzle as shown which agitates the mixture and induces air into the stream, thus forming a mass of small air bubbles with similar characteristics to the foam produced in the chemical

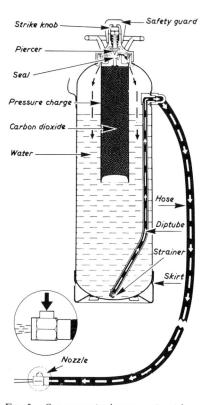

FIG. 5.—*Gas pressurized water extinguisher.*

extinguisher. This is referred to as "mechanical or air foam'"*, the stabilizing substance in this case being usually a protein compound derived from dried blood. The ratio of foam to liquid is about 8:1, not quite so good as for "chemical foam".

4.2.5. Carbon Dioxide Extinguishers.

The CO_2 portable extinguishers found on board ship will usually be in accordance with BS 3326 : 1960 "Portable Carbon Dioxide Fire Extinguishers", this specification covering extinguishers containing not less than 1 kg (2 lb) and not more than 7 kg (15 lb) of CO_2 when filled to a filling ratio of 0·667. The filling ratio is defined as the ratio of the weight of liquefiable gas in the cylinder to the water capacity of the cylinder at 15°C (59°F).

---

* If it is found that the difference between mechanical foam and chemical foam is difficult to understand: a mechanical foam may be made by vigorously agitating a soapy solution, a chemical foam may be made by taking a soapy solution and stirring therein a spoonful of health salts.

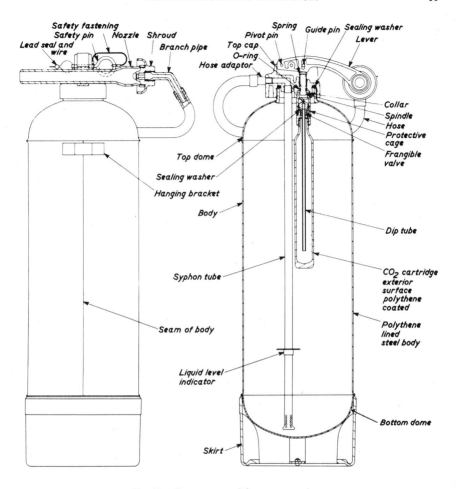

FIG. 6.—*Gas pressurized foam extinguisher.*

The figure of 0·667 has regard to the high pressure commensurate with the tropical temperatures which ships are likely to encounter.

Carbon dioxide is classed as a high pressure, liquefiable gas and when stored under pressure in the liquid state at ambient temperature necessitates the use of high duty steel cylinders. These are usually constructed for a working pressure of 136 bar (1980 lb/in²) and are hydraulically tested to 207 bar (3000 lb/in²) or more depending on the standard to which they are constructed.

The means for operating modern extinguishers of this type fall into two classes, namely, the piercing of a disc or the opening of a valve. Each method of operation has its merits and drawbacks. The operation of the disc type, when initiated, cannot be stopped and hence although a small fire may be quickly put out, the extinguisher must be permitted to continue discharging until empty. On the other hand, this very feature ensures that, as is possible with the valve operated type, a partially empty extinguisher is not returned to its rack after use and possibly become a hazard to the next man who seeks to use it in the belief that it is fully charged. The discharge from the valve operated type can, of course, be stopped at will but it is imperative that any partially discharged extinguisher be so marked until the opportunity arises for it to be fully charged again.

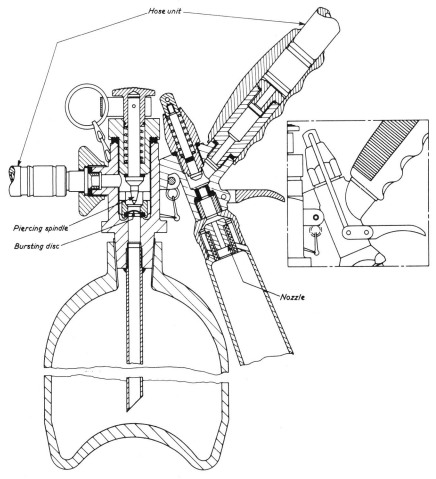

FIG. 7. (a)—*Liquid CO$_2$ extinguisher—diaphragm type.*

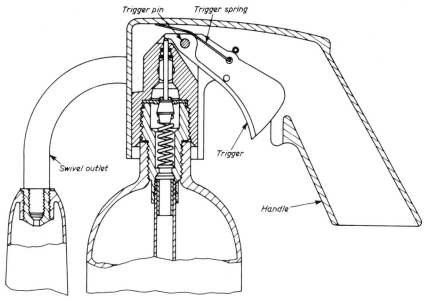

FIG. 7. (b)—*CO$_2$ extinguisher—valve type.*

In either case, the liquid is discharged through a short flexible or swivel hose to a discharge horn, where the liquid changes to a gas and is spread evenly over the burning surface, thus excluding the air. An internal pipe is fitted to ensure rapid release of liquid so that the evaporation will not take place in the bottle as this would cause icing due to the extraction of latent heat causing the formation of solid CO_2. Figures 7(a) and (b) show typical extinguishers of these two types; a 4 to 5 kg (10 lb) charge produces about 2 to 3 m^3 (90 ft^3) of gas, which has a good blanketing effect, but only a small cooling effect. These high pressure bottles are not allowed in accommodation spaces because of the danger of gas leakage which, if confined might suffocate crew or passengers. 3 kg (7 lb) CO_2 extinguishers may be substituted for 9 l (2 gal) foam extinguishers in the machinery spaces, the advantage of gas being its cleanliness and its ability to penetrate into otherwise inaccessible spaces. Being a non-conductor of electricity it may be used on fires involving electrical appliances. The weight of the liquid is small however compared to the total weight which has to be carried around and there is no visible check on leakage so that bottles have to be weighed regularly to see that they are in good order. Furthermore, they can only be recharged ashore.

4.2.6. Dry Powder Extinguishers

Another extinguisher which is very useful on chemical fires and is accepted on a limited basis in accommodation and machinery spaces is the dry powder type, the relevant British Standard Specification being BS 3465 : 1962 "Dry Powder Portable Fire Extinguishers". Two basic types are to be found and to quote verbatim from the Standard ". . . the dry powder is expelled by means of pressure resulting from compressed gas from pressure container (gas cartridge) attached to or fitted into the extinguisher or from compressed gas or air stored with the powder in the body of the extinguisher". Figure 8 illustrates a typical example of one such type. The

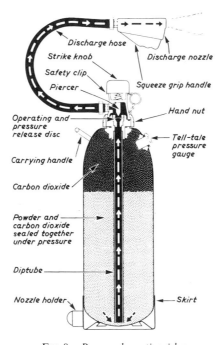

FIG. 8.—*Dry powder extinguisher.*

body may be made of steel or aluminium and is designed with a factor of safety of 4, the working pressure being defined as the closed nozzle pressure for the gas cartridge type, and the stored pressure for the stored pressure type. The standard once again lays down maximum and minimum discharge times for the sizes of extinguisher and for the 4·5 kg (10 lb) size—accepted in the United Kingdom as the equivalent of a 9 l (2 gal) foam or soda–acid type, depending on the type of powder used—the relevant times are 10 and 15 sec. A 6 kg (13 lb) extinguisher of the stored pressure type would contain about 220 g (about 8 oz) of dried CO_2.

Actuating the extinguisher results in the powder charge, usually sodium bicarbonate, potassium bicarbonate or ammonium phosphate, depending on the class of fire for which it is intended, being blown out of the extinguisher body usually through a hose which may have a controllable nozzle. A free flowing agent, such as magnesium stearate, is added to avoid compacting of the powder. The internal gas tube is arranged to give a violent motion inside the container to induce the powder into the stream of gas. The action of this powder is a little difficult to explain. It commences by blanketing the fire in a cloud thereby excluding the air, and continues by interrupting the chain reaction of combustion from one burning molecule to another, but as the discharge is very rapid, being completed in about 15 sec, the success of the operation requires accuracy in application.

In the case of sodium bicarbonate, if the fire is hot enough it will decompose to form sodium carbonate, water and carbon dioxide, and although some authorities say that this carbon dioxide has little effect on the fire, about $4\frac{1}{2}$ ft^3 gas/lb of powder is produced so it should have an extinguishing effect. Powder charges in which (typically) ammonium phosphates or sodium chloride form the base chemical, extinguish fire by fusing on the surface and thereby excluding air—hence their use against specific hazards such as carbonaceous or metallic fires. Although there are many new types of extinguisher, powder in this connexion is not a new material, for its use as a fire extinguishing medium was very popular before the First World War. Later, it suffered almost a total eclipse after evidence was given before a special committee that "these powders are of no more value than so much sand and are less effective than a bucket of water". This view was quoted in 1923 by a Royal Commission on Fire Brigades and Fire Prevention which advised that the use of the powders was not to be recommended. However, the improved types appear to be very effective on fires involving carbonaceous materials, flammable liquids, gases and even metals, depending on the powder used, but as there is no cooling action with this type of extinguisher, speed of action on finding a fire is essential if success in extinguishing it is to be achieved.

Whilst it is debatable whether or not a dry powder extinguisher is equally efficacious as one of the foam or soda–acid types, it has to be admitted that a disadvantage is its lack of cooling effect. However, be this as it may, it is only relevant when talking of fires involving carbonaceous or liquid substances as fires involving gases are preferably to be tackled using such extinguishers. When refilling them, it is essential to ensure absolute dryness of the powder and the container. Finally, it is interesting to note that the British Standard specification for dry powder extinguishers is the only specification among those dealing with portable extinguishers which categorically states what the extinguisher shall be capable of doing. In essence the extinguisher shall be capable of extinguishing in still air conditions, after a 30 sec pre-burn, a petrol-on-water fire in a tray having an area of 0.14 m^2 ($1\frac{1}{2}$ ft^2) for each 0.45 kg (1 lb) of powder in the extinguisher and containing 101 petrol/m^2 ($\frac{1}{4}$ gal/ft^2) of tray area.

4.2.7. Halogenated Hydrocarbon Extinguishers

These types of fire extinguishers will only be briefly mentioned as although small extinguishers containing certain media in particular are accepted for use in specific situations, they are in general banned from ships coming within the scope of the 1965 Rules.

Halogenated hydrocarbons belong to a class of fire extinguishing agents known as vaporizing liquids and are derived from hydrocarbons, such as methane, which have had some or all of their hydrogen atoms replaced by the halogens, i.e. fluorine, chlorine, bromine and iodine. Further information on them is contained in Section 6.9. They act, in part, by forming a blanket of gas which will not support combustion over the fire but, of more importance, they have a reverse catalytic action on the chain reactions taking place in the flames and this plays a major part in extinguishing the fire. However, the exact mechanism by which this is achieved has not been positively established.

Of the group of fire extinguishing media which come within the generic term of halogenated hydrocarbons, probably the most well known is carbon tetrachloride (CTC). However, carbon tetrachloride and others, such as methyl bromide, while being efficient fire extinguishing media, have fallen out of favour principally on account of the unacceptable level of toxicity of the liquid before and/or after pyrolisis and are not permitted on British ships. More efficient and less toxic extinguishing media have however been developed, e.g. bromochlorodifluoromethane (BCF) and bromotrifluoromethane (BTM), sometimes known, respectively, as Halon 1211 and Halon 1301; these are accepted to a limited extent. Thus on British ships, small BCF and BTM portable extinguishers may be found in such positions as radio rooms and switch boards, the familiar 1 quart CTC extinguisher, well known to the older engineer, now being banned as stated due to the tendency of the liquid after pyrolisis to form phosgene, a toxic gas.

4.3. NON-PORTABLE EXTINGUISHERS

Some of the portable extinguishers described so far, in particular the foam, CO_2 and dry powder types also come in larger sizes. The gross tonnage and class of ship, power and type of main propelling machinery determine whether or not a 45·5 l (10 gal) or 136 l (30 gal) capacity foam extinguisher is provided in the machinery or boiler spaces, 16 kg (35 lb) and 45 kg (100 lb) carbon dioxide extinguishers being deemed acceptable alternatives. Unlike their smaller counterparts, there are no British Standards specifications which cover the construction and performance of these non-portable extinguishers, but some guide lines in this respect are contained in the Rules. Thus, in the case of the foam type, whilst the range of 14 m (45 ft) and period of discharge (not less than 100 sec) are laid down for the 136 l (30 gal) capacity machine, no requirement is made in respect of method of operation, the designer thus being left free to develop this aspect as he pleases.

Providing the fire main is always pressurized, a foam making hose reel

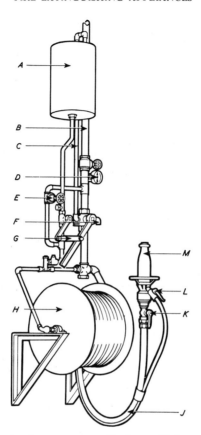

A. *Foam-making compound tank.*
B. *Water supply from pump.*
C. *Air pipe into tank top.*
D. *Pressure gauge.*
E. *Scouring valve.*
F. *Air intake.*
G. *Interconnected lever opening air, compound and water cocks.*

H. *Removable hose reel.*
J. *Coupled water and compound hoses.*
K. *Branchpipe water cock.*
L. *Branchpipe compound cock.*
M. *Foam-making branchpipe.*

FIG. 9.—*Foam hose reel unit.*

unit such as is illustrated in Fig. 9 is acceptable in machinery and boiler spaces in lieu of a 136 l (30 gal) non-portable fire extinguisher. The type illustrated is intended for bulkhead mounting and incorporates its own foam compound supply tank (A). Lever (G) operates three cocks simultaneously, one controlling the water supply from the fire main, one controlling the foam compound tank vent to atmosphere and the third controlling the supply of compound from the tank. On opening lever (G) in addition to venting the tank to atmosphere and opening the supply valve from the tank, water flows to one inlet on the side of the hose reel, the other inlet receiving a solution of water and foam compound, the compound having been induced into the water stream by means of an inductor unit. The hose reel contains a length of twin hose, secured together as shown, the reel end of each hose being attached to one of the side inlets referred to. To the free ends of the hoses is attached a foam making branch pipe where the two solutions mix and, with the addition of entrained air, produce foam. Foam quality is controlled by the operation of levers (L) and (K). Water pressure in excess of 41 bars (60 lb/in^2) is usually necessary before such equipment can be used effectively. As speed of action is essential if success is to be achieved in fighting an incipient fire, this type of equipment is extremely useful under the conditions stated, as by the mere opening of one valve foam is readily available at the nozzle without the need to have previously un-wound the hose. After use, the foam compound tank should be refilled immediately, and the foam compound hose and connexions washed through with clean sea water by using scouring valve (E).

In the carbon dioxide types of non-portable extinguishers, it is essential in view of the pressures involved to lay down the specification to which the cylinders must be constructed i.e. BS 401 : 1931, BS 1287 : 1946 or BS 1288 : 1946, the Home Office Specification "S" being accepted as an equiv-alent. Other features, such as rate of discharge which affects performance, and means to prevent injury to the operator from electrical discharge or cold burn on discharge of the extinguisher are specified but once again the method of operation is left to the ingenuity of the designer. Although termed non-portable, these extinguishers are usually mounted on wheels for ease of movement. The use of these larger non-portable machines is usually resorted to after several portable extinguishers have been used to no avail. In such circumstances, no hesitation should be permitted in using these larger appliances as a machinery space fire which is not extinguished after several portables have been expended, may now be travelling in all directions and any oil which is involved has had several minutes pre-burn time, a dangerous situation. Far better to "over-kill" the fire with massive appli-cations of foam or other extinguishing medium than risk using more portables only to find the conflagration is now beyond the extinguishing capability of the non-portable equipment system and the attendant necessity of aban-doning the machinery space in question.

Non-portable dry powder extinguishers have been fitted in machinery spaces, usually at the owner's request, but the result of discharging such an extinguisher in a relatively confined space should not be forgotten. Although the fire that necessitated its discharge may be put out, the resulting "fog" may in its turn be indirectly responsible for injury to personnel through loss of vision and it is considered that such equipment is more suitable for use in open spaces, such as on deck in LPG (liquid petroleum gas) and LNG (liquid natural gas) ships and at the loading manifold of a tanker.

FIRE EXTINGUISHING APPLIANCES

Although only protein foam has been referred to up till now, it may be of interest to note at this point that two other types of foam, namely fluoro-protein foam and aqueous film forming foam (AFFF) are beginning to find favour in the marine world in view of their superior flame knockdown and faster fire control capabilities. The former is a combination of hydrolized protein and fluorosurfactant usually in a 3–10 per cent concentration in water, depending on method of application and equipment used, while the latter is a synthetic foam, in a 6 per cent concentration in water, with the unique ability of extinguishing oil fires by allowing water to float on the fuel thus providing an effective vapour seal.

5. FIRE ALARM AND DETECTION SYSTEMS

5.1. INTRODUCTION

An automatic fire alarm and detection system is required to be installed in the cargo, accommodation and service spaces of certain classes of passenger ships and in the cargo spaces of ships carrying explosives. Such systems are also fitted in the machinery spaces of cargo ships specially designed for unmanned operation and on the vehicle decks of certain roll-on, roll-off ships depending on the conditions of carriage of the vehicles. Deliberations at IMCO may well result in a fire alarm and detection system being included in one method of structural fire protection in cargo ships.

Fire detectors operating on various different principles are currently available and the types presently found in service on board ship will be included in the following list:

1) heat detectors which operate at a predetermined temperature;
2) heat detectors which operate when the rate of temperature rise of the surrounding air reaches a set limit;
3) smoke detectors which operate when smoke obscures a beam of light falling on a photoelectric cell;
4) smoke detectors which operate when a beam of light is scattered by smoke and caused to fall on a photoelectric cell;
5) combustion products detectors which operate when an electric current flowing through an ionized atmosphere is changed;
6) flame detectors which react to radiation emanating from flame;
7) the sprinkler system also incorporates an automatic fire alarm and detection system but this will be described in the section dealing with fixed fire extinguishing systems.

Other types of fire detectors are available such as line detectors, laser beam detectors, etc. but space does not permit the description of more than the six types listed.

5.2. HEAT DETECTORS

5.2.1. Fixed Temperature Type

The current British Standard Specification under which this type of detector may be manufactured is BS 3116:1970 Part I "Automatic Fire

Alarm Systems in Buildings". Although this is a specification basically for land use, it is convenient to accept and use it for marine applications as well.

The means of operation is extremely simple usually being either a bi-metallic strip or a soldered joint. In the first type, the bi-metallic strip is used to make or break an electric circuit at a pre-set temperature. When it is arranged to make a circuit, the contacts are usually encapsulated in a glass cover to avoid the contacts becoming affected by the atmosphere since any corrosion may prevent the passage of current when the contacts are required to make a circuit.

The second type may consist of two electric contacts joined through light springs, by low melting point solder. Thus, when the air temperature reaches the melting point of the solder, the joint pulls apart under the action of the spring and the alarm is sounded. Other types using the same principle, i.e. the making or breaking of an electric circuit by the action of melting solder are available; Fig. 10 shows one such type.

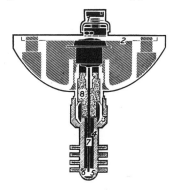

1. *Connecting terminal.*	5. *Insulating pip.*
2. *Socket assembly.*	6. *Finned case.*
3. *Plug assembly.*	7. *Central conductor.*
4. *Fusible alloy.*	8. *Insulating bush.*

FIG. 10.—*Fire detector—fixed temperature type.*

Heat detectors incorporating bi-metallic strips are especially useful in such places as boiler rooms where rapid variations of temperature are likely to be encountered and preclude the use of the rate-of-rise type detector described later. The soldered type of detector is seldom found on board ship due to various factors which include the impracticability of routine testing and possible effects of the marine environment on solder.

5.2.2. Heat Detectors of the Rate of Rise Type

As with the previous type, the relevant BS specification is BS 3116: Part I : 1970. This type of detector works on the principle that providing the rate of increase in the temperature of the surrounding air is above a given minimum, the detector will operate between given time limits, the latter depending on the rate of increase of temperature. Both fixed temperature and rate of detectors, constructed in accordance with the British Standard specification referred to, are required to have response times in accordance with the graph in Fig. 11 reproduced from the standard. Detectors of this

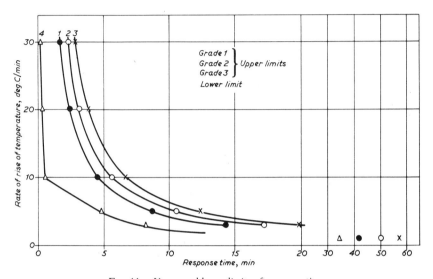

FIG. 11.—*Upper and lower limits of response time.*

type may be of Grade I, Grade II or Grade III but as this standard has only recently superseded BS 3116 : 1959 which did not grade detectors according to response performance, most of the detectors presently available have only been tested to the earlier specification. The response times of heat sensitive detectors depend on various factors among which is the height the detector is situated above floor level. As the size of fire to which a detector will respond increases considerably with the height of the deckhead on which it is mounted, the Grade I detector is more suitable for higher deck-heads; also in unattended machinery spaces any heat sensitive detector to this specification should be of a Grade I type, on account of its faster response time. It is of interest to note that the standard also requires all detectors made in compliance with it to actuate at a given temperature, according to its grade, when the rate of increase in temperature is very small. Thus, in effect, this type of device now incorporates the fixed temperature characteristic of the previously described detector.

Referring to Fig. 11, the reader may wish to know that for any given rate of rise of temperature the detector to be acceptable must operate between the left hand curve (4) and one of the other three depending on its grade. Whereas it is fairly obvious that if the response time lies to the right of the curves 1, 2 or 3 the detector is not sensitive enough, it is not immediately apparent why the detector is also unacceptable if the response time lies to the left of curve 4. All marine engineers are familiar with the attitude of mind that false alarms engender and it is for this particular reason, i.e. to avoid over-sensitivity that curve 4 has been introduced.

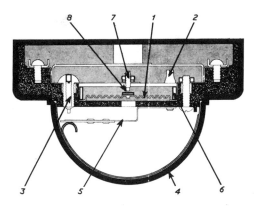

1. *Diaphragm assembly.*
2. *Breather valve.*
3. *Fixed temperature adjustment screw.*
4. *Dome assembly.*
5. *Contact spring.*
6. *Diaphragm mounting ring.*
7. *Rate of rise adjustment screw.*
8. *Silver contacts.*

Fig. 12.—*Fire detector—rate of rise (pneumatic) type.*

Two typical ways of effecting the required result are illustrated. In Fig. 12 a pneumatic type is shown in which an otherwise sealed chamber is fitted with a bleed-off orifice. Means for permitting expansion of the chamber due to increase in temperature are provided so that when a predetermined limit of movement is reached, an alarm is sounded. Thus, under normal diurnal and nocturnal changes of temperature the bleed-off hole will be able to exhaust and inhale air such that the alarm condition is never reached. Under the action of rapid heat input under fire conditions however, the air expands faster than it can exhaust through the bleed-off orifice, the resulting expansion ultimately sounding the alarm.

Figure 13 shows a thermal type of detector which works on the bi-metallic strip principle. It consists essentially of two such strips, one insulated from rapid changes of temperature and the other although enclosed being exposed to such changes. Contacts on the ends of the strips form part of an electric circuit. Thus, on slow rise of temperature due to say normal climatic conditions, the heat input to both strips is similar and hence the contacts remain apart. On rapid increase in temperature, the unprotected

1. *Electrical connexion*
2. *Fixed temperature stop.*
3. *Gold plated contacts.*
4. *Shielded bi-metallic element.*
5. *Unshielded bi-metallic element.*
6. *Aluminium cap.*
7. *Plastic base mounting.*

FIG. 13.—*Fire detector—rate of rise (bi-metal strip) type.*

strip responds more quickly than the insulated strip with the result that the contacts meet and the alarm sounds.

5.3. SMOKE DETECTORS

5.3.1. Light Obscuration Type
No British Standard Specification presently exists for this type of detector and hence there is no standard in respect of performance. A detector incorporating the light obscuration principle is shown in Fig. 14.

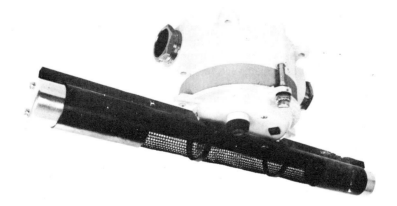

FIG. 14.—*Smoke detector—light obscuration type.*

In this particular type, a beam of light is arranged to fall on a photo-electric cell and if the atmosphere between the light source and cell is clear, the balance of the electrical circuit is not disturbed. On smoke passing, by convection across the detector however, the intensity of light falling on the photo-electric cell is reduced, the change in the electrical output being used to operate an alarm at a predetermined level.

As greater sensitivity can be obtained by utilizing what is known as the Tyndall effect, detectors of the light obscuration type are being gradually superseded by detectors of the light scatter type described below.

5.3.2. Light Scatter Type

When a beam of light traverses a transparent medium, e.g. air, its intensity is reduced by absorption and partly by scattering. The latter arises from some kind of heterogeneity in the medium, the most obvious ones being due to suspended particles such as smoke, dust or liquid particles. This light scattering property is often called the Tyndall effect after the physicist of the same name who pioneered the work in this field.

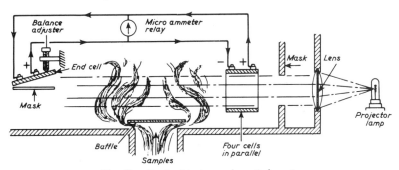

FIG. 15.—*Smoke detector—schematic layout.*

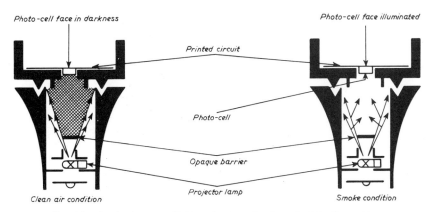

FIG. 16.—*Smoke detector—light scatter type showing principle of operation.*

Two diagrammatic arrangements of smoke detectors which utilize this principle are shown at Figs 15 and 16. As can be seen from an inspection of Fig. 16 the beam of light is prevented from illuminating the photo-electric cell by a light barrier. The surrounding atmosphere circulates through the detector head by virtue of the normal air currents and providing no dust or smoke particles are present in it, the electrical balance of the detector circuitry remains undisturbed. On smoke entering the detector however, the light rays are reflected or scattered around the light barrier and reach the photo-electrical cell, the change in current being used to signal the alarm condition.

Another type is shown in Fig. 15 where a parallel beam of light is caused to pass through inwardly facing photo-electric cells. The inside of the chamber is matt black and the cells referred to only receive a small amount of stray light. The light also falls on an end cell mounted obliquely to the beam and so angled that balance of the circuit is obtained. On smoke entering the chamber, the intensity of the light falling on the end cell is decreased and that received by the inwardly facing cells increased by reason of the deflexion of the light beam by smoke particles, the inbalance in the circuit being arranged to signal the alarm condition.

Disadvantages of detector heads using photo-electrical cells and lamps are obvious, e.g. failure of the lamp filament, gradual falling off in performance of the photo-electrical cells, susceptibility of both to vibration, etc. but modern day circuitry can be arranged that in such an eventuality the equipment "fails safe" and registers the fault condition in the circuit.

This is particularly important when such a fire detecting arrangement is used in connexion with a system which draws air samples from several spaces simultaneously and passes the composite sample through the single head, as failure of the detector renders the whole system inoperative. The sensitivity of the detector in this case, of course, must be extremely high as any smoke emanating from any one sampling pipe is diluted by the air issuing from the remainder.

5.4. COMBUSTION PRODUCTS TYPE DETECTOR

Most of the detectors of this type use two ionized chambers in series, as shown in Fig. 17. One of the chambers is open to the surrounding atmosphere while the other is enclosed. The atmosphere in both chambers is ionized by a radioactive source, elements such as americium and radium being used. The ionization of the atmospheres in the two chambers under normal conditions permits a minute current to flow, caused by the positive and negative ions, created by the radiation, moving in opposite directions Fig. 18. The supply voltage across the two chambers is therefore divided, a common connexion being taken from the central point to a cold cathode tube. On the products of combustion, which may even be too small to be seen by the naked eye, entering the outer chamber the tendency is for them to collect ions by collision and as the "aerosols", as they are known, are

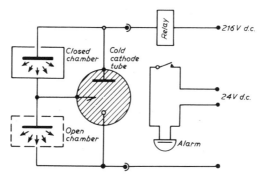

FIG. 17.—*Basic detector circuit.*

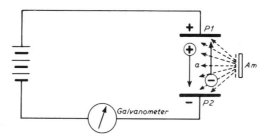

FIG. 18.—*Principle of the ionization chamber.*

much larger than the ions, the latter are virtually stopped by the collision. A reduction in the ion flow obviously means a reduction in the voltage across the chamber and hence a change in the voltage at the common terminal. The latter, as stated, is connected to the trigger electrode of a cold cathode tube, so arranged that on a predetermined voltage level being reached, the tube "fires" and permits the passage of a small current, sufficient to activate an alarm relay. The alarm will continue to sound until such time as the electrical power is removed, this permitting the tube to return to its initial state.

The sensitivity of this type of detector can be varied by altering the levels of radiation in the chambers or by altering the voltage necessary to "fire" the cold cathode tube.

Such a detector is most suitable for use in machinery spaces and can be adjusted to a high level of sensitivity especially when unmanned operation is required and where prompt detection of fire is imperative. However, this very feature is to some extent a disadvantage as false alarms can occur when the sensitivity is too high; too many false alarms produce a loss of confidence in the equipment. It is worth while noting here that this type of detector does not depend on the combustion products being visible; it is the number of particles that is important. Thus, a large number of particles, although they may be invisible will cause the indicator to go to the alarm condition while a smaller number of particles, which may be in the form of smoke, may not necessarily do so. From a more practical point of view, the presence of steam, in the outer chamber will activate this type of detector and it is important to site them well clear of any steam leak-off, e.g. turbine glands.

5.5. Detectors which react to Radiation Emanating from Flame

Detectors of this type can be of the infra-red or ultra-violet light type but up to now it is only the former type which is being used in ships. These detectors are intended to respond to radiated heat and light, and to avoid false alarms being given by natural or artificial light, they have been designed to respond only to that particular part of the spectrum which is character-istic of flame. Heat radiating from hot machinery will therefore not affect this type of detector. The circuitry of the system is also arranged such that the detector will not go to the alarm condition when immediately sensing radiation, e.g. the striking of a match to light a cigarette or pipe, but only if the radiation persists for a pre-determined time.

One obvious, drawback of such detectors is that if smoke screens the detector from the fire before the detector has an opportunity of sensing it, its operation is unlikely. Another disadvantage is the possibility of the detector reacting to light being received from a vibrating source—this, of course, can be catered for by careful siting during installation.

With the above mentioned drawbacks in mind, these radiation type detectors are seldom, if ever, used by themselves but always in company with types previously mentioned.

In conclusion, it is considered that a fire detector system for use in machinery and for boiler spaces should ideally consist of, in the main, smoke or ionization type detectors, backed up by one or two infra-red type de-tectors so sited as to survey as much as possible of the protected space, and one or more thermal detectors of the rate of rise type for use in such spaces as boiler rooms.

It goes without saying that such intricate equipment is valueless if it is not regularly serviced and tested and the aspiring professional engineer is well advised to be *au fait* with the practicalities of the system in his ship, if not with the intricate electronics involved.

6. FIXED INSTALLATIONS

6.1. INTRODUCTION

Any crew member may come across a fire in its early stages before the fire alarm system, if fitted, has operated and by prompt and intelligent action, using the portable or non-portable extinguishers immediately to hand (depending on where the fire is), he can avert a major conflagration. If the fire is in the machinery spaces and has gained a strong hold, the use of the larger and more complicated fixed fire extinguishing system may ultimately be necessary, but in view of the necessity for abandoning and closing down the affected space, these would only be resorted to on the authority of the master or chief engineer.

Such an operation would generally be carried out under the supervision of one of the more senior engineer officers, but this is no excuse whatsoever for the junior or uncertificated members of the engineering staff not being familiar with the particular system fitted in their ship. It is also in his best interests to be equally familiar with the fixed fire extinguishing systems fitted in other parts of the ship external to the machinery spaces. Descriptions of the various systems available are given below, reference being made to the types of ship and spaces therein for which they are suitable.

6.2. WATER SPRAY SYSTEMS

6.2.1. Accommodation and Service Spaces

The accommodation and service spaces of a cargo ship are not required to be fitted with any form of fixed fire extinguishing system although a certain amount of structural fire protection is required under the Merchant Shipping (Cargo Ship Construction) Rules 1965. Improved methods of structural fire protection in cargo ships are presently under consideration at IMCO though.

Passenger ships of certain classes however, when built to Method II construction, referred to in Part V of the Merchant Shipping (Passenger Ship Construction) Rules 1965, or in fact, to one of the alternatives referred to in Chapter H of the International Convention for the Safety of Life at sea 1960, are required to have an automatic sprinkler and fire alarm system fitted for the detection and extinction of fire in all spaces in which a fire may be expected to originate, and a typical sprinkler system is shown on the left

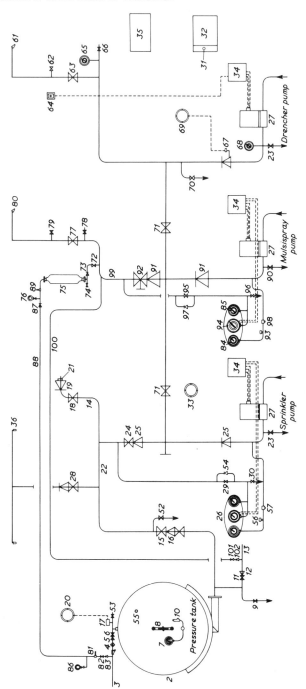

2. *Pressure tank.*
3. *From ships air supply.*
4. *Union with restricted air supply.*
5. *Check valve* } *on air supply.*
6. *Stop valve* } *on air supply.*
7. *Pressure gauge.*
8. *Water level indicator* } *pressure tank.*
9. *Drain valve* } *pressure tank.*
10. *Safety valve.*
11. *Stop valve* } *fresh water supply.*
12. *Check valve* } *fresh water supply.*
13. *From ships fresh water supply.*
14. *Shore connexion.*
15. *Stop valve* } *pressure tank.*
16. *Check valve* } *pressure tank.*
17. *Low air alarm switch.*
18. *Stop valve* } *shore connexions.*
19. *Check valve* } *shore connexions.*
20. *Pressure tank alarm bell.*
21. *Hose coupling.*
22. *Trunk main.*
23. *Pump test valve.*
24. *Pump delivery stop valve.*
25. *Pump delivery check valve.*
26. *Automatic pressure relay.*
27. *Pump*
28. *Installation control valves.*
29. *Automatic relay isolating valve.*

30. *Release valve.*
31. *Indicator pilot lamp.*
32. *Indicator.*
33. *Sprinkler alarm bell.*
34. *Automatic pump starting panel.*
35. *Diagram of ship.*
36. *Sprinklers.*
52. *Trunk main drain valve.*
53. *Air release valve (pressure tank).*
54. *By-pass check valve.*
55. *Fusible plug.*
56. *Alarm for pump running.*
57. *2-way cock.*
61. *Drenchers.*
62. *Drain valve.*
63. *Drencher control valves.*
64. *Remote start push button.*
65. *Pressure gauge.*
66. *Air release valve.*
67. *Alarm pressure switch (drencher).*
68. *Pressure gauge.*
69. *Drencher alarm bell.*
70. *Trunk main drain valve.*
71. *Interconnecting valve (locked shut).*
72. *Stop valve (mulsispray).*
73. *Check valve.*
74. *Drain valve (for air vessel).*
75. *Air vessel.*

76. *Pressure gauge (air vessel).*
77. *(Mulsispray) control valve(s).*
78. *Air release.*
79. *Drain valve.*
80. *Mulsisprayers.*
81. *Safety valve.*
82. *Stop valve.*
83. *Check valve.*
84. *Pressure gauge (pump delivery).*
85. *Pressure gauge (main).*
86. *Pressure gauge (air line to air vessel).*
87. *Check valve (air vessel).*
88. *Air line.*
89. *Fusible plug.*
90. *Pump test valve.*
91. *Pump check valve.*
92. *Pump stop valves.*
93. *(Diaphragm alarm switch).*
94. *Automatic (pressure relay).*
95. *Automatic gauge isolating valve.*
96. *Release valve.*
97. *By-pass check valve.*
98. *2-way cock.*
99. *Mulsispray main.*
100. *Fresh water feed.*
101. *Stop valve.*
102. *Check valve.*

FIG. 19.—*Diagrammatic arrangement of sprinkler, mulsispray and drencher systems.*

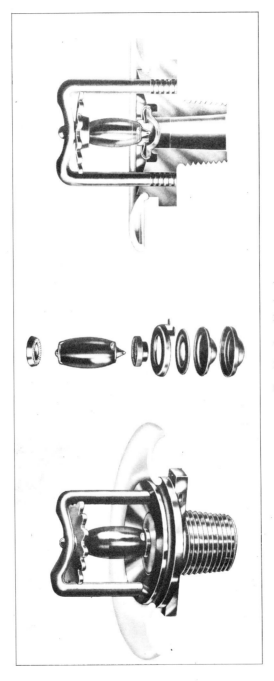

Fig. 20.—Sprinkler head.

hand side of Fig. 19. This incorporates a number of sprinkler heads (one type being shown in Fig. 20) which are supplied with water under constant pressure, and so arranged that every part of each space requiring protection is adequately covered. Each head has a glass or quartzoid bulb which retains a diaphragm seal in the outlet of the water pipe. This bulb is partially filled with a special fluid so arranged that a rise in temperature in the compartment concerned will cause the liquid to expand. When the liquid has expanded and entirely filled the space, the bulb, being unable to withstand further pressure, bursts, the water pressure forces the diaphragm out, and water flows from the sprinkler. The usual temperature at which the bulb bursts is 155°F but special bulbs are available to burst at 79°C and 93°C (175°F and 200°F) for operating in hotter parts of the ship. Under the specific pressure of 5·5 to 8·3 bars (80 to 120 lb/in²) maintained in the reserve tank by air pressure the water from the sprinkler is deflected upwards and outwards and broken into a fine spray by the serrated edge of the sprinkler base and will adequately cover a floor area of 12 m² (169 ft²). As the pressure falls to the lower figure, the salt water pump starts automatically. Each installation is divided into convenient sections, generally containing not more than 200 sprinkler heads and each section has a control valve as shown in Fig. 21. When a sprinkler head comes into operation water pressure lifts the non-return valve thereby gaining access to the annular ports normally covered by the valve face. This allows pressure to build up in the alarm system and operate the trip switch, causing the alarm to sound on the bridge and indicate the section concerned. For testing purposes a small valve is incorporated, and when this is opened it allows the same flow through the valve as a sprinkler head and confirms that the alarm system is in good order. This method may also be used to give the alarm if a small fire is discovered before the sprinkler heads come into operation. The control valve must be open at all times except when sprinkler heads are being replaced so it is either locked open or has an electric alarm to show if it is inadvertently shut. The system is charged initially with fresh water to prevent corrosion, but the pump naturally supplies sea water so that when the system has been operated it must be drained, flushed through and refilled with fresh water. The system should be tested each week and to avoid contaminating the standing fresh water charge with sea water each time, a drain valve is fitted in the pump discharge line. By opening this valve and shutting the cock at the pressure operated switch and the pump discharge valve, the pump can be allowed to cut in automatically as required and discharge to the bilges.

6.2.2. Machinery Spaces

The machinery spaces of certain cargo and passenger ships—depending on the type and horsepower of the machinery and the vessel's size and class —are required by law to be fitted with a fixed fire extinguishing system, a choice of basic types being permitted. The water spray system is one such

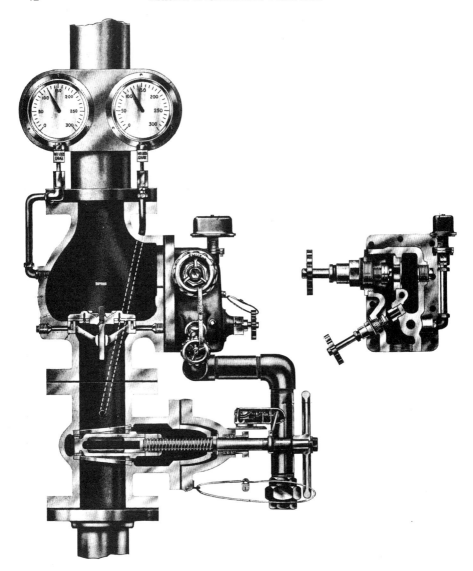

FIG. 21.—*Control valve.*

type and the centre of Fig. 19 shows such a system for a passenger ship, cross connected to the sprinkler system provided for the protection of the accommodation and service spaces and the drencher system referred to later.

The main difference between the machinery space water spray system and the sprinkler system is that whilst the sprinkler system is automatic in operation, the former requires to be manually operated. The sprayer head is similar to the sprinkler head but has no glass bulb, different types of deflector base being used to vary the spray pattern as required.

The system is pressurized by fresh water, pressure being maintained to the section control waves (77) at all times. An air vessel is incorporated into the system to prevent the pump (under the control of a pressure switch) cutting in when there is only a slight leakage of water. When the section control valve is opened, water is supplied to the various sprayer heads fitted over, for example, bilges, tank tops and other areas over which oil may spread, and to other main fire hazard areas. The system may be divided into zones so that water need only be directed on to those areas involved in a fire.

As is to be expected, the pump and its controls are positioned outside the space and the arrangements are such that a fire in the protected space cannot put the system out of action.

The system should be tested regularly but the efficient execution of this may be more easily said than done. The possibility of water spraying over electrical equipment and wiring while the ship is on passage is something which the professional marine engineer will avoid at all costs; consequently a section of the system is often sought for testing purposes which may be operated without fear of the consequence. Once this is found, it is only too easy to assume that if the system is tested satisfactorily on the section in question, then the remaining sections of the system are equally efficacious. It is suggested that this complacency is the very attitude which must be discouraged if a high level of confidence in the ship's fire fighting capability, backed by actual testing, is to be maintained. Every effort should be made to vary the sections tested. Where an air line connexion is provided, the pipework and sprayer heads can be proved clear by blowing through with compressed air but the automatic operation of the pump can only be demonstrated by actual test. It goes without saying that the external source of power to the water spray system (probably the emergency generator) and the mobile hand sprayers provided should be included in the periodic testing.

6.2.3. Cargo Spaces

In passenger ships, the use of water spray systems outside the machinery and accommodation spaces is almost exclusively used for the protection of vehicle decks in roll-on, roll-off ferries where access to the deck is required and a smothering gas system is therefore inappropriate. Whereas the strict letter of the law requires A60 fire divisions to be fitted in vehicular decks, the nature and purpose of the latter precludes their provision and a water spray system has long been accepted as an alternative.

Prior to 1965, a normal sprinkler system as fitted in the passenger accommodation, together with arrangements for providing, at intervals not exceeding 40 m, a thwartship water curtain spraying over a 1 m prohibited parking zone, was basically accepted as being satisfactory, but progress and experience has shown that a modified sprinkler system, commonly called a drencher system, is preferable and superior. This latter system then is the one generally fitted on all new passenger vehicular ferries built in the last few years and eliminates the spray curtain and 1 m prohibited parking zone referred to above, the observance of which was difficult to maintain and whose efficacy was always a bone of contention. Such a system is shown on the right hand side of Fig. 19.

In effect, the system consists of a distribution network of pipes, supplied with water from a drencher pump, and to which are connected open drencher heads. The system covers the vehicle deck and is divided into zones, the minimum length of which is related to the length of the longest vehicle presently permitted on European roads. Each zone is controlled by its own valve and the pump capacity is such that at least the two longest adjacent zones can be supplied simultaneously at their rated capacity. Thus, irrespective of where a long vehicle is parked, all parts of it are within the range of the drencher heads. The latter are similar to those used in machinery spray systems in that no glass bulbs are fitted, their spacing and application rate being governed by the deck head height. Thus, when the deck head height is 2·5 m or more, the spacing of the heads requires to be such that a water application rate on to the deck of $5·0 \, l/m^2/min$ is possible and when less than 2·5 m, the rate is reduced to $3·5 \, l/m^2/min$.

The system is manually controlled and, hence, a fire has to be actually discovered before any action to combat it can be taken. However, such action does not require the drencher pump to be so started, as opening the control valve to any zone automatically starts the pump in question. From the foregoing, it is obvious that the periodic testing of the drencher system presents no problems, the sequential testing of the system, two zones at a time, being proof positive that the system is fully operational. It also serves to demonstrate that the drainage arrangements, essential from a stability point of view on a deck so protected against fire, are clear and in good order.

6.3. FOAM SMOTHERING SYSTEMS

6.3.1. Low Expansion Foam Systems

A foam smothering system to the boiler room or engine room may use either chemical or mechanical foam. In older ships there may be chemical foam supplied from storage tanks on the upper deck containing larger quantities of solutions similar to those used in the portable foam extinguisher. When these are allowed to mix by opening a valve, the formation of CO_2 produces bubbles in the stabilizer liquid and builds up the pressure necessary to eject the foam through open ended pipes over the boiler room or engine room tank tops, the quantities being arranged so as to give about 150 mm (6 in) depth of foam over the areas to be protected. This type of operation has fallen out of favour however and has not been installed in ships for a number of years.

The foam systems installed today are generally of the types shown in Figs. 22, 23 and 24 and rely on the formation of "mechanical foam" by mixing foam-making liquid with water in the ratio of about 3 to 5 per cent and by violent agitation in the presence of air to create air bubbles in a tough skin of foam. The compound used for making mechanical foam usually has a protein base and such low expansion foam has an expansion ratio of about 6:1 to 8:1.

In the system shown in Fig. 22, two tanks are used containing fresh water and foam-making liquid, respectively. The water can be ejected by the release of carbon dioxide or nitrogen from storage bottles, and in its passage across an "induction" fitting, draws the required proportion of foam-making liquid from the second tank. The mixture then flows along pipes to the machinery and boiler spaces, but before it is released it passes through nozzles in special foam-making fittings (Fig. 25) where it is agitated and entrains the air necessary for the formation of foam. This system is easy to operate, and produces the pressure necessary to form the optimum amount of foam. By the addition of extra CO_2 cylinders and foam compound however, additional protection may be obtained, but it must be remembered that the water to fill the storage tank must come from a source external to the space being protected, e.g. from the emergency fire pump. The system shown in Fig. 23 has the foam-making liquid stored in a tank with connexions to a large bore water main. When the water supply,

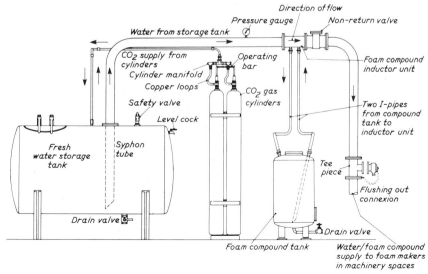

FIG. 22.—Mechanical foam installation—self-contained pressurized type.

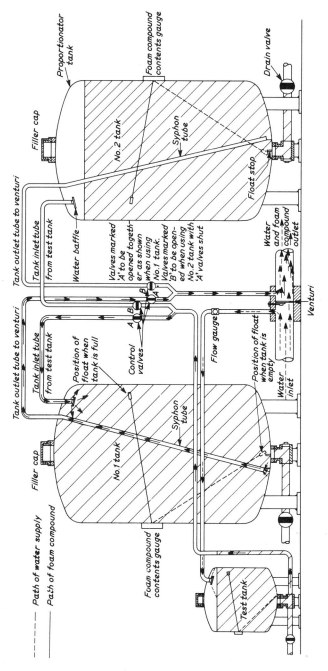

FIG. 23.—Mechanical foam installation—pump type.

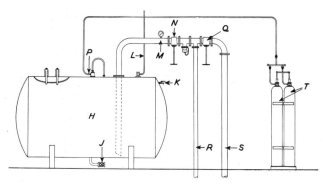

H. *Solution storage tank.*
J. *Drain valve.*
K. *Level cock.*
L. *Safety valve.*
M. *Pressure gauge.*
N. *Stop valve.*
P. *CO₂ supply from cylinder.*

Q. *Distribution valve.*
R. *Solution supply to branchpipe in machinery space.*
S. *Solution supply to foam makers in machinery space.*
T. *CO₂ cylinders.*

Fig. 24.—*Mechanical foam installation—"pre-mix" foam pressurized type.*

which must have a connexion to the emergency fire pump, is pressurized, the foam-making liquid is induced into the system by the reduction in pressure resulting from the water flowing through a venturi. This mixture is then carried along to a foam-making fitting (Fig. 25) and the foam generated therein is distributed from open ended pipes. With this type of system it is also possible to use a hand foam distributor by attaching a hose and a

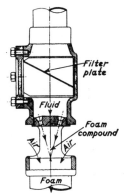

Fig. 25.—*Foam making fitting.*

special foam-making nozzle into the main distribution line. Similar portable foam-making nozzles, which can be coupled to a fire main and take their foam liquid supply from a portable tank, are also available and a sectional drawing of one such type is shown in Fig. 26. Arrangements can be made

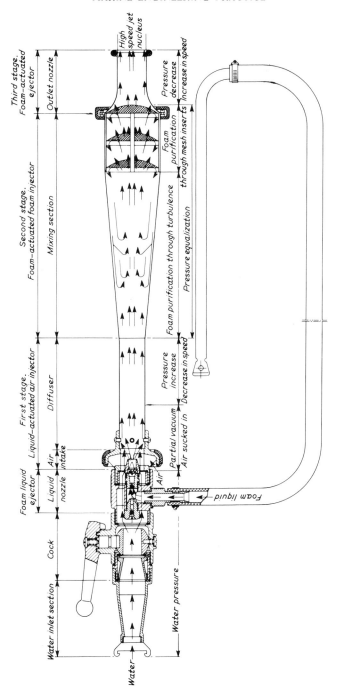

FIG. 26.—Portable foam making nozzle.

for foam to be discharged on to equipment above the floor plates where a fire hazard exists, and to vary in consistency so that it will even adhere to a vertical surface. At the same time, outlets below the floor plates should be so arranged that there are no obstructions in the way of the free flow of foam across the tank top. These systems are very sensitive to the water pressure available, very little foam being produced below 2 bars (30 lb/in²) at the nozzle, whilst the recommended pressure of 5 bars (75 lb/in²) is not often available on ships' firemains. A variation of this arrangement is shown diagrammatically in Fig. 24 in which the foam compound and water are mixed in solution and stored in tank (H). The tank, as in the system shown in Fig. 22, can be pressurized by the release of CO_2 cylinders (T), the solution being directed as required, through pipe (R) to the hand held branch pipes, or through pipe (S) to the foam making spreaders in the machinery or boiler space. Although only one pipe (S) is shown, the system can be divided into sections each with its own stop valve. Distribution and application of the foam can thus be made on a more selective basis and can result in a more efficient and economic use of the foam available.

A more sophisticated system is shown in Fig. 27 in which an automatic inductor unit is placed in the suction line to the fire pump. A small proportion of the water discharged from the pump is by-passed into the inductor

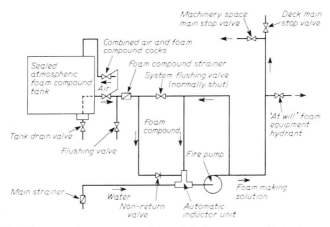

FIG. 27.—*Diagrammatic arrangement of automatic foam compound induction system.*

unit to supply the inductor jet. The venturi effect of the jet creates a vacuum in the inductor port which draws in foam compound from the tank, the solution of water and compound then being discharged into the fire pump suction line. The induction of this solution is controlled by sensing the flow of water in the suction line, the sensor operating a metering valve which increases the flow of foam compound as the water flow in the main increases and *vice versa* in the desired ratio.

The foam compound tank need only be sufficient for its purpose, i.e. it is not a pressure tank, and is sealed from the atmosphere to prevent deterioration of the contents. The air vent and supply valves are linked so that it is impossible to open the latter without the former, thus positively preventing inadvertent maloperation.

To operate the system, only the combined air and foam compound cocks need be opened and the fire pump started, the automatic induction unit then varying the amount of compound used in accordance with the demand.

A modified version of this system is shown in Fig. 28 in which a foam compound pump is added. This pump draws compound from the tank and delivers it to the automatic induction unit which controls the amount of compound injected by mechanically sensing the main water flow.

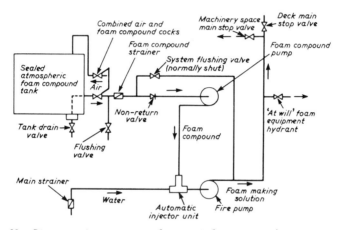

FIG. 28.—Diagrammatic arrangement of automatic foam compound injection system.

The tank and pump may be placed in any convenient space (outside the protected space) the only considerations being convenience of putting the system into operation and the frictional losses in the foam compound pipework between tank, pump and injector unit.

It will be obvious that the fire pumps supplying the water in Figs. 27 and 28 require to be outside the protected spaces as indeed does the foam compound pump shown in the latter figure. Whilst the sequence of operations are simple, it must be remembered that the starting of the fire and compound pumps, if electric, will involve the starting of the emergency generator if protection of machinery spaces is involved.

A major problem associated with the use of low expansion foam as a fire fighting system in machinery spaces is that it is most effective only in the horizontal plane. Such a capability is ideal where the burning oil is conveniently held within areas bounded by save-alls but, unfortunately, the most dangerous fires are those involving burst fuel lines higher up in the space. The released oil can be ignited by steam lines, hot surfaces like high pressure turbines, exhaust manifolds of diesel machinery, electric motors, etc. and few of these potential sources of ignition are protected by this system. Testing of the foam system too presents a major difficulty because few, if any, ship's engineers could accept the disruption caused by having to clean out the foam which is a difficult and messy task. Yet without such testing there is no guarantee that the system will operate when required. After use it is important to wash through the system with fresh water, particularly those which incorporate an automatic induction unit which has a propensity to "gum-up" if left. Some of these foam systems, particularly those protecting both machinery spaces and tank decks, are quite complex in layout and it is important that all officers on board clearly understand the operation of the installation.

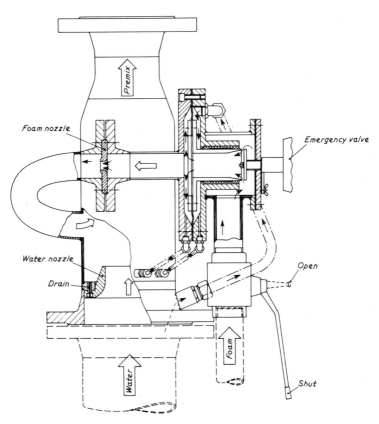

Fig. 29.—*Automatic proportioning valve.*

6.3.2. Deck Foam Systems on Tankers

Although all cargo vessels over 2000 gross tons are required to have their cargo spaces protected by a fixed fire extinguishing system which discharges the fire extinguishing medium within the said spaces, Rule 32(1) of the Merchant Shipping (Fire Appliances) Rules 1965 permits a fixed foam system in lieu of the above to be fitted on the deck of a tanker i.e. external to the cargo space. Such a system is primarily intended to combat fire resulting from deck spillage of cargo but is unlikely to prevent fire and explosion within tanks.

Fixed deck foam systems use low expansion foam which is usually of the protein base type when designed for use with petroleum cargoes immiscible with water. The foam may be produced by one of the systems previously described and illustrated in Figs. 23, 27 or 28, i.e. a water/foam

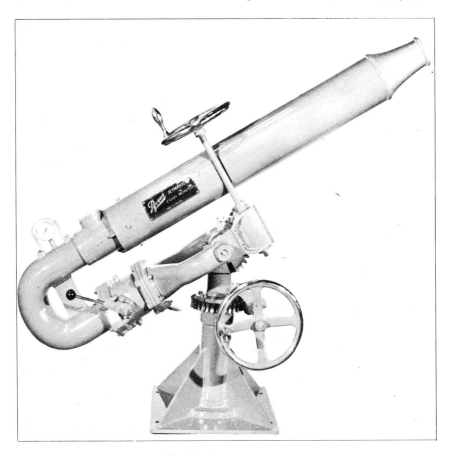

FIG. 30.—*Foam monitor.*

compound solution is piped along the deck. Alternatively, the foam may be manufactured at the monitor itself, i.e. separate water and foam compound lines run the length of the deck and each monitor has a connexion to each main. A drawing of a typical mixing valve used in the latter system is shown at Fig. 29.

The monitors are usually sited on the centre line of the ship, their spacing being such that one monitor is within the range of the next. Thus, the whole deck area can be covered with foam supplied by monitors, hand applicators giving flexibility of operation during the final stages of fighting a fire and for delivering foam, as required, into intact or ruptured tanks. The design of the monitor does not have to comply with any statutory regulations but usually it is arranged to have a 360° horizontal traverse, a jet altitude of up to about 60 to 70° above the horizontal and may be locked in any desired position. Figure 30 shows a typical monitor used on board a modern tanker.

The Rules referred to require that a deck foam system shall be capable of supplying 50 mm (2 in) of foam over the whole tank deck area in 15 min. Greater capacity than this is usually provided however, the whole question of foam application rates presently being under the active consideration of the Sub-committee on Tanker Safety of IMCO in which the U.K. is represented.

6.3.3. High Expansion Foam Systems

The systems referred to earlier use low expansion foam but high expansion foam, i.e. foam having an expansion rate of up to 1000:1 is also available for use in both fixed systems (excluding deck foam systems on tankers) and for portable equipment. Its generation and method of distribution are quite different from that of the low expansion foam systems already described and although high expansion foam has not been used to any great extent in British ships, it has great potential and it is considered that a review of the foam systems available would not be complete without a description of it.

The production of high expansion foam necessitates the use of a special foam generator which consists essentially of a power driven fan, a net or gauze, a supply of high expansion foam compound and a means to spray the water/foam solution evenly over the net. Figure 31 illustrates such a generator, the external shutter (4) being provided to protect the net from the heat of the fire before it can be wetted.

The operation of the generator is as follows. Foam solution is uniformly sprayed over the net, which is usually made of nylon, and air is blown through it. On opening the external shutters, foam of uniform size and having an expansion of up to 1000:1 is produced and ducted away to the protected space.

The foam is tough and persistent and is an excellent insulator and absorber of radiant heat. On such a foam reaching a fire, unit volume of

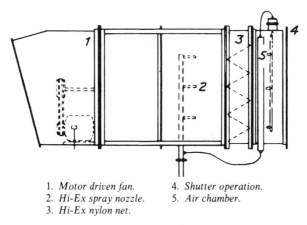

1. *Motor driven fan.*   4. *Shutter operation.*
2. *Hi-Ex spray nozzle.*   5. *Air chamber.*
3. *Hi-Ex nylon net.*

FIG. 31.—*High expansion foam generator.*

water in the foam is turned into approximately 1700 volumes of steam, the resulting atmosphere now containing only approximately $7\frac{1}{2}$ per cent by volume of oxygen, far less than the percentage required to sustain burning. At the same time, the surrounding foam prevents access of further oxygen to the fire.

The ducting for the distribution of high expansion foam has, of necessity, to be of large cross section and this to a certain extent militates against its use due to the paucity of space in a modern engine room and pump room. High expansion foam also has the tendency to break down when passed through long lengths of ducting. The preferred arrangement is therefore to arrange for the main ducts to end at about engine room crown level, the foam then falling to the bottom of the space, and to provide additional ducts where practicable, to cover the major fire hazards. A froth generating capacity which will allow the level of the froth discharged to rise at about 1 m/min is generally regarded as acceptable.

Some authorities consider that it is possible for a person, caught in space filled or filling with high expansion foam, to be able to breathe by clearing the foam from the front of his face and effect his escape providing he has been trained for such a contingency and does not panic. Others entirely repudiate the idea except under very favourable circumstances. The authors are of the opinion that in the Merchant Service as a whole, where no such training is given, and having regard to the size and/or complexities of modern machinery space arrangements, such action should not be attempted; rather, emphasis should be placed on ensuring that all personnel are accounted for before filling with high expansion foam is commenced. However, the possibility is well worth remembering if by chance one is caught in the situation envisaged. While little damage is caused by the foam to equipment not damaged by the fire, it should be borne in mind that an extended period of time may elapse before the machinery space can be re-occupied as the foam has either to be washed away with water spray or allowed to decay naturally, a time consuming operation.

Latest developments in the use of such foam include the possibility of inerting the cargo spaces of oil tankers and combination carriers during water washing procedures to reduce the risk of explosion but such an application is still in the development stage, as is the use of inert gas in producing the foam.

6.3.4. Medium Expansion Foam

Although not found yet to any great extent in British ships, systems using medium expansion foam are available. The expansion of the foam is of the order of from 75:1 to 150:1 and its distribution is usually by hand held applicators, the water supply coming from the fire main and the foam concentrate from portable drums. An in-line inductor, to which the foam concentrate supply and fire main are connected ensures that a solution of the correct proportions is delivered to the applicator for converting into foam of the correct expansion ratio. One such type is illustrated in Fig. 32.

It is of interest to note that foam having an expansion ratio of from 50:1 to 150:1 has been accepted in principle by the IMCO Sub-Committee on Fire Protection for use on the decks of tankers.

FIG. 32.—*Medium expansion foam-making branchpipe with in-line inductor.*

6.4. Carbon Dioxide Smothering Systems

6.4.1. General

Carbon dioxide, on account of its fire extinguishing efficiency, cleanliness and ease of application, is the most common fire smothering gas used in fixed systems on board ship, steam long having fallen out of favour. CO_2 is a non-flammable, colourless, odourless, slightly acid gas and is approximately $1\frac{1}{2}$ times as dense as air. Its specific volume at $21 \cdot 1°C$ ($70°F$) and 1 bar is $8 \cdot 76$ ft^3/lb which, for practical purposes, is rounded up to 562 l/kg ($9 \cdot 0$ ft^3/lb) when calculating the weight of gas required, for a given volume of cargo or machinery space, to comply with the Rules. Its critical temperature is $31 \cdot 0°C$ ($87 \cdot 8°F$) above which temperature it cannot be changed into the liquid state by the application of increasing pressure.

For many years, when used for fire extinguishing purposes, CO_2 has been stored in steel cylinders to an appropriate British Standards or Home Office specification. However, with the growing increase in the size of ships, the appearance of new types of ships designed for specific trades, e.g. car carriers, and the increase in CO_2 concentrations required by various statutory authorities when certain cargoes are carried, systems in which the gas is stored in a single pressure tank under refrigeration and hence at a much lower pressure than when stored in steel cylinders were devised and are now firmly established on the marine scene.

6.4.2. Carbon Dioxide Cylinder Systems

The cylinders most commonly used nowadays are those manufactured to BS 1288 : 1946, "Manganese Steel Gas Cylinders for Carbon Dioxide, Nitrous Oxide and Ethylene", and Home Office Specification "S". The cylinders have internal pipes fitted which permit the CO_2 to pass through the distribution pipework to the nozzles in the liquid state and it only evaporates on discharge from the nozzle (Fig. 33). The internal pipe therefore

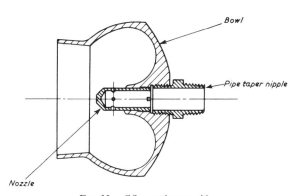

Fig. 33.—CO_2 nozzle assembly.

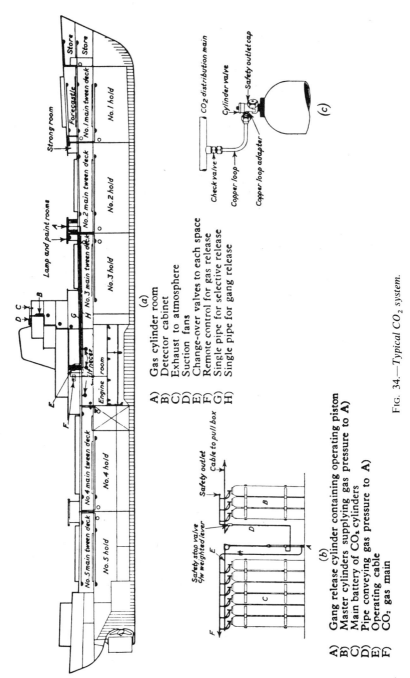

A) Gas cylinder room
B) Detector cabinet
C) Exhaust to atmosphere
D) Suction fans
E) Change-over valves to each space
F) Remote control for gas release
G) Single pipe for selective release
H) Single pipe for gang release

A) Gang release cylinder containing operating piston
B) Master cylinders supplying gas pressure to A)
C) Main battery of CO₂ cylinders
D) Pipe conveying gas pressure to A)
E) Operating cable
F) CO₂ gas main

FIG. 34.—Typical CO₂ system.

prevents evaporation of the liquid taking place on operation of the system, as the resultant drop in pressure and temperature would cause the vapour to freeze and deposit as snow in the valve and pipework.

The cylinders are grouped together in banks in the CO_2 room as shown in Fig. 34 (b). The outlet valve of each cylinder discharges through a connecting pipe into a common manifold (F), a non-return valve being incorporated into the connecting pipe in order that the cylinder may be disconnected from the header, for replacement purposes, without loss of pressure. The connecting pipes are usually of copper but increasing use is being made of flexible connexions on account of ease of installation. The CO_2 in the header then passes to a sector valve situated in a control cabinet, supplying the machinery space distribution pipework and may also be connected to a series of 3-way cocks, or double-seated valves (E), Fig. 3.4 (a), supplying the various cargo holds. This part of the system is described later. For machinery space extinguishing systems, speed of operation and a fast rate of delivery are essential and hence the cylinders which are to be used for this purpose are arranged for simultaneous operation of the cylinder valves in all but the smallest systems, "pilot" or "master" gas cylinders (B) in Fig. 34 (b) being used to activate a gang release system.

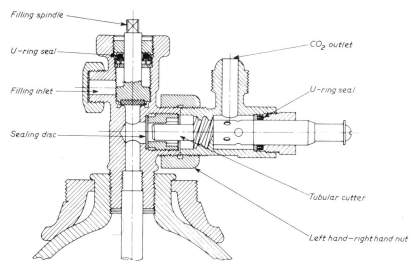

Filling spindle

U−ring seal

Filling inlet

Sealing disc

CO_2 outlet

U−ring seal

Tubular cutter

Left hand−right hand nut

FIG. 35.—CO_2 cylinder head valve.

Three typical types of cylinder head valve are shown in Figs. 35, 36 and 37, and whilst they differ in detail, they are all capable of being remotely operated. Also, the method by which the ultimate aim, i.e. the release of the gas, can be achieved varies and two different systems are shown diagrammatically in Figs. 34 (b) and 38 to illustrate just how different they can be.

Figure 34 (b) shows a bank of cylinders with the head valve levers connected together, usually by phospher bronze wire, the free end of the latter being attached to the piston in a gang release cylinder (A). The handles of the head valves of the master gas cylinders (B) are similarly connected together, the free end of that connecting wire terminating in a handle in the control cabinet referred to above. The control cabinet door is usually locked, the key being sited adjacent to it in a glass fronted box. The control cabinet door incorporates a switch controlling an alarm in the machinery spaces, personnel therein therefore receiving prior notice of any intention to discharge gas into the space. In the interests of safety it is most desirable for the sector valve or cock within the control cabinet to be so arranged that it is impossible to close the cabinet door with the valve or cock in the open position. The gas discharge from the pilot cylinders is led to the operating cylinder (A). To operate the system, the control cabinet door is opened thus sounding the machinery space alarm. The machinery space sector valve is opened and the operating handle pulled to open the head valves on the master cylinders. Gas from the latter, on entering the gang release cylinder (A), pushes the piston down thus operating all the cylinder head

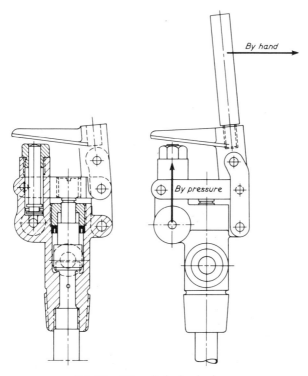

By hand

By pressure

Fig. 36.—*CO_2 cylinder head valve.*

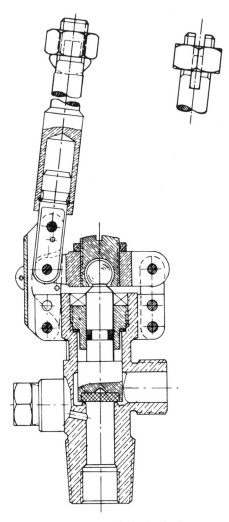

FIG. 37.—CO_2 cylinder head valve.

valves coupled together. Gas then flows into the machinery space via the CO_2 main, sector valve and various distributors.

In Fig. 38, a diagrammatic arrangement is shown of a pressure operated CO_2 system designed for the protection of machinery spaces.

The control cabinet door, as before, has an alarm switch (11) incorporated into it, but instead of concealing a manual pull control it now conceals one or more gas cylinders (14) and two control valves (15) and (16). A pressure gauge (17) enables the operator to check that adequate pressure

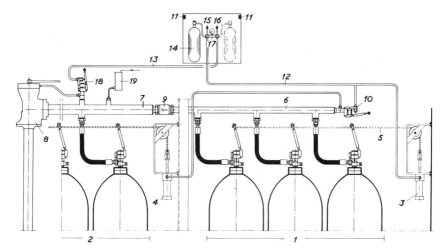

1. *Pilot cylinders.*
2. *Main battery cylinders.*
3. *Pilot cylinder pressure operated release mechanism.*
4. *Main battery cylinder pressure operated release mechanism(s).*
5. *Connecting wire.*
6. *Pilot cylinder manifold.*
7. *Main battery cylinder manifold(s).*
8. *Main valve (pressure operated).*
9. *Non-return valve.*
10. *Main battery cylinder release control valve.*
11. *Switches for alarm and ventilation stop.*
12. *Control line No. 1.*
13. *Control line No. 2.*
14. *Master cylinder(s).*
15. *Master control valve No. 1.*
16. *Master control valve No. 2.*
17. *Manometer.*
18. *Control valve, main valve opening.*
19. *Pressure operated switch.*

FIG. 38.—CO_2 *(pressure release) system.*

is available for starting the system. Operation is as follows, assuming cylinder valve (14) is open. On opening valve (15), the pilot cylinder pressure operated release mechanism (3) is caused to operate, which opens the pilot cylinder head valves (1) by means of connecting wire (5). Valve (10) also opens simultaneously permitting the gas pressure in main (6) to activate the main battery release mechanism (4), thus opening the main cylinders (2) to the main battery manifold (7). On opening valve (16), valve (18) is caused to open, permitting gas pressure from manifold (7) to open the sector valve (8) which is held shut by the gas pressure. In the unlikely event of this valve not opening, a manual means is provided for jacking the valve open. Gas then flows to the distribution pipework in the machinery space.

Precautions should be taken before the gas is released in both the above systems to ensure that all skylights and ventilators are closed and fans and oil pumps are stopped for these are one shot systems. No chances can be taken of the gas being dispersed or re-ignition taking place. It is imperative to ensure that all personnel are evacuated from the space before the gas is released on account of its suffocating effect.

Although only required by statute in specific circumstances, the CO_2 system using cylinders to holds and storage spaces usually has a detecting system incorporated. The pipes used to convey the carbon dioxide to the various spaces are interrupted, at convenient places, and a special double seated valve or cock referred to previously is placed in each line. A pipe leading from the space above the valve is taken with similar pipes from other lines to a detecting cabinet and thence to an extractor fan.

When the valve is screwed down, the fan extracts samples of air from each cargo or storage space, and this is passed through the cabinet where lighting is so arranged that smoke coming through any line is easily detected. If required, a light sensitive cell can be arranged to ring an alarm when the smoke interrupts the light falling on it. Should a fire be detected, the appropriate double seated valve is opened to its full extent—this closes the pipe to the detector cabinet and opens the line from the storage bottles to the space concerned. Gas can then be supplied as required by opening individual bottles by hand (Fig. 34(c)) until the atmosphere in the space has been made sufficiently inert to extinguish the fire. Provided that the gas can be retained in the space, it is very effective but again all ventilation and dispersal of the gas should be prevented.

It is important in the case of a fire in a hold not to discharge at the outset the contents of all or even too many cylinders and the manufacturer's instructions should be followed. Factors which have to be taken into account include permeability of the space, i.e. how densely is the cargo packed and how much space can be occupied by the gas and what is on fire, e.g. baled cotton or loose rubber tyres. The distance and estimated time to reach a suitable port with shore fire fighting facilities dictates the time interval between discharge of the number of cylinders available for topping-up purposes. Topping-up with gas is absolutely essential because inevitably there is, in spite of a rigid control of ventilation, slight leakage of gas which has to be replaced.

The system should be checked through periodically when the holds are empty; some ships have an air connexion allowing each line to be blown through in turn; or a single bottle of gas can be used to prove that all the lines are clear. The detecting unit can be checked by holding a smoke generator or smouldering piece of rag beneath a diffuser in each space in turn, and having someone check that the smoke can be seen at the right position in the cabinet. It was hitherto usual to weigh the bottles regularly to see that they held the correct amount of liquid, but a new method has been developed using a radio-active isotope and a detector which can show the difference in the amount of radiation passing through the liquid as opposed to that passing through the gas space above, and thereby indicates the level of the liquid inside. Its operation is limited to temperatures below the critical temperature of CO_2 as it is impossible to change the gas to liquid above this temperature as stated earlier; in practice its use is restricted to 27°C (80°F).

6.4.3. Bulk Carbon Dioxide Systems

A bulk CO_2 fire extinguishing system consists essentially of one or more pressure tanks, refrigerating machinery and the appropriate network of pipes for distributing the gas around the machinery or cargo spaces. It is of interest to note that when used for the latter spaces, the system does not usually incorporate a fire detection system as is possible, and usual, with the cylinder system. No reason is seen why such a facility could not be adapted into the system if required however.

The pressure vessel is of Class I construction, a typical steel being to BS 1501/224 Grade 32A, with low temperature properties to $-50°C$ ($-58°F$). All welds are fully radiographed. Although, when the system was first introduced, it was usual to provide 2×100 per cent Rule capacity tanks, experience, confidence and economics have now resulted in a single CO_2 tank of Rule capacity, albeit adequately equipped with alarm devices to detect incipient leakage, being accepted. The tank is heavily insulated and covered with metal cladding, the working temperature and pressure being $-20°C$ ($2°F$) and 21 bars ($300\,lb/in^2$). Internal cooling coils are connected to dual refrigerating units, the latter being controlled automatically by pressure switches. Filling and vapour return lines are provided for dockside servicing; blanks are fitted over the end flanges of these lines on completion of filling and carefully checked to ensure they are gas tight. Instrumentation in addition to the usual pressure gauges includes a double means of ascertaining the contents, a loss of capacity alarm and alarms to detect leakage past the main liquid discharge valves.

A flow diagram for a typical bulk CO_2 fire extinguishing system is shown in Fig. 39. The means for warning personnel in the machinery spaces that gas is about to be released has not been shown but does not differ from that provided in the cylinder system, e.g. alarm switches on control cabinet doors, limit switches on machinery space sector valves, etc. Operation of the system in case of fire is self evident and merely requires the appropriate valves to be opened in the correct sequence.

The tank and its instrumentation should be examined regularly and once per day is suggested. Contents gauges should be checked to ensure no leakage has taken place since the last inspection, the means for checking the tightness of the relief valves usually being to secure rubber balloons over the ends of the waste pipes. Any inflation of the balloon tells its own story. The relief valves are usually designed specially for use with CO_2, an illustration of one being given in Fig. 40. Contrary to normal steam practice, any means for lifting the valve off or turning it on its seat are usually omitted since frequent and conscientious testing of the valves not only loses gas but may result in the valves actually leaking because of CO_2 ice crystals becoming jammed between valve and seat. It goes without saying that any noticeable loss of tank contents, or operation of one of the built-in safeguards, should be ceaselessly investigated until such time as the cause is positively ascertained and rectified, if possible.

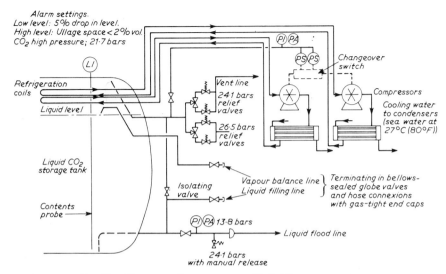

FIG. 39.—*Diagrammatic arrangement of bulk CO_2 storage system.*

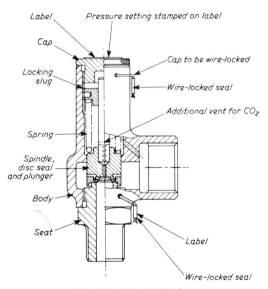

FIG. 40.—*CO_2 relief valve.*

6.5. INERT GAS GENERATORS

To cater for the risk of re-ignition or of a fire occurring after all the gas in the CO_2 system just described has been used, a system for producing inert gas in large quantities on demand has been developed and is shown in

Fig. 41. The system is not permitted for the statutory protection of machinery spaces, however, as the time lag in reducing the oxygen percentage in the affected space is unacceptable from fire fighting considerations.

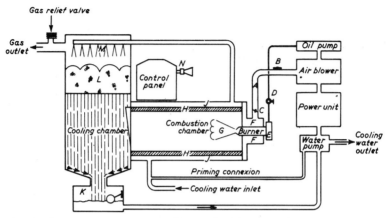

A. *Air duct.*
B. *Air relief valve.*
C. *Butterfly valve air regulator.*
D. *Oil fuel governor valve.*
E. *Oil fuel regulator.*
F. *Air space.*
G. *Flame.*

H. *Fire-brick lining.*
J. *Water jacket.*
K. *Float chamber with high level water switch.*
L. *Lessing ring labyrinth.*
M. *Water sprayer.*
N. *Alarm for flame or water failure.*

FIG. 41.—*Diagrammatic arrangement of inert gas generator.*

A measured amount of fuel is fed to a combustion chamber and ignited with the correct amount of air to give perfect combustion, the exhaust gas having a high CO_2 content of about 14 per cent (by volume) and a low O_2 content of about 1 per cent, the remainder being N_2. The combustion chamber is pressurized at from 0·3 to 0·6 bars (4 to 8 lb/in²) so that after passing through a specially arranged washing and cooling chamber, where excess carbon and sulphur gases are removed and the temperature is reduced, the gas flows to a distribution manifold, from which it can be released to any space as required. This system may also be arranged for the detection of incipient fire in the same way as a stored CO_2 system. Owing to the low gas pressure, the distribution pipes are rather large, but the gas generator can run as long as fuel and water are available. Units with capacities of up to 15 000 nominal m³/h are available to comply with the requirement that the generator should supply gas to fill the largest compartment in four hours. The pumps, air blowers and other auxiliaries are usually independently driven by a diesel engine or by an electric motor coupled to the main and auxiliary generators, whilst it is also possible to use a small gas turbine for this purpose. This inert gas system should be tested once a week; its main disadvantage is the large diameter of the distribution pipes required, though if the pressure in the system could be raised, then the size of these pipes could be reduced.

6.6. Funnel Gas Inerting Systems

A system in which gases taken from the boiler uptakes are washed, cooled and blown by fans, at a slight pressure, into the cargo spaces of tankers has, for some years, been accepted as an alternative to the fixed fire extinguishing systems specifically mentioned in the Merchant Shipping (Fire Appliances) Rules 1965. It is a condition of acceptance that irrespective of whether the ship is loading, transporting or discharging cargo, washing empty tanks or merely travelling in ballast, the particular operation must be carried out under a blanket of inert (i.e. oxygen-deficient) gas. The intention and purpose of the system is to prevent the ingress of air into a tank containing flammable hydrocarbon gases as the resulting mixture may well fall within the flammable range of the gases in question. As stated elsewhere in this paper, providing one side of the "fire triangle" is removed (air, fuel, means of ignition), fire becomes impossible and this is what this system seeks to establish by the removal of the first named.

To date, funnel gas systems have only utilized the exhaust gases from boilers, as the exhausts from compression ignition engines contain too high a percentage of oxygen, especially on light load. They can however be adapted for such duty by the use of after burners. A more consistent and better quality gas is obviously obtained when the boiler is under automatic control and in this respect, the IMCO Sub-committee dealing with the fire protection of tankers has not only accepted the philosophy of inerting cargo tanks as a means of preventing tank explosions, but has also spoken to the necessity of the boilers supplying the gas being controlled automatically. A typical composition of a funnel gas would be 12 to 14 per cent CO_2, 2 to 4 per cent O_2, 0.3 to 0.5 per cent SO_2, with N_2 making up the balance.

A diagrammatic arrangement of a typical inert gas system is shown in Fig. 42. The cargo tanks in the design shown are connected to a common deck main (21) having the gas inlet at one end and the pressure/vacuum valve (27) and by-pass valve (28) at the other.

Gas is taken from the boiler uptakes (1), via isolating valves (2) to the scrubbing tower (3) where it enters under a water seal in the base. Water sprayers in the top of the tower are supplied from pumps (4) and (5). The gas is drawn up the tower, where the SO_2 is washed out, through a water separator to the fans (10) where it is blown through the deck water seal (15) to the inert gas main (21). A recirculating line (12) is provided.

The deck water seal is situated aft on the open deck and consists of a tank into which the gas is passed through a water seal in the base. Both this seal and the one in the scrubbing tower ensure that there can be no reversal of flammable gas flow back into the fans, or, more seriously, into the boiler uptakes. The length of vertical pipe through which the gas enters the deck

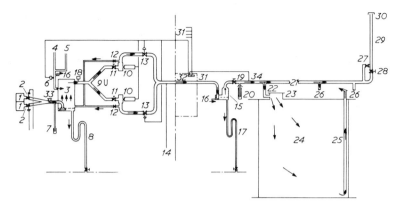

1. *Boiler uptakes.*
2. *Boiler uptake valves, remotely controlled from soot blower panel or Engine Control Room or position.*
3. *Scrubbing tower.*
4. *Sea water supply from independent pump.*
5. *Sea water supply from general service pump.*
6. *Pressure stat or flow meter alarm and to stop blower on water failure.*
7. *Scrubbing tower flooding tell tale.*
8. *Overboard effluent line.*
9. *Test manometer.*
10. *Blower and motor. Remote start/stop from Control Room.*
11. *Blower suction isolating valve.*
12. *Blower discharge recirculating line.*
13. *Pneumatically operated valve which closes when blower fails or is stopped or on scrubber water failure. Valve will control vapour main pressure by setting of Pumproom sited controller.*
14. *CO_2 indicators. Two boiler indicators alarm at 10 per cent and below.*
15. *Deck water seal.*
16. *Sea water make up supply to deck water seal.*

17. *Overboard discharge from deck water seal.*
18. *Temperature switch to stop blower on high gas temperature.*
19. *Deck isolating valve.*
20. *Oil filled pressure and vacuum breaker.*
21. *Deck vapour main.*
22. *Branch lines to tank hatch coamings.*
23. *Tank hatch.*
24. *Cargo tank.*
25. *Purge pipe.*
26. *Branch line to each cargo tank.*
27. *Pressure and vacuum relief valve and flame screen.*
28. *P. & V. by-pass valve.*
29. *Mast riser.*
30. *To atmosphere.*
31. *Pneumatic pressure transmitter lines to gauges in Engine room; Pumproom entrance: cargo control room and on the bridge.*
32. *Pneumatic controller for modulating blower discharge control valve.*
33. *Blower fresh air intake.*
34. *Sensing point connexion for pneumatic pressure transmitter.*

FIG. 42. *Diagrammatic arrangement of typical inert gas system.*

seal is usually designed so that before any back pressure in the tanks could force the water in the seal back to the blowers, the deck oil-filled pressure vacuum breaker (20) and/or pressure–vacuum valve (27) would have operated and relieved the pressure. From the deck seal, the gas passes through an isolating valve into the deck main to which all cargo tanks have connexions (22). A common mast riser (29) incorporates the pressure/vacuum valve (27) referred to, the operating pressures being about 0·14 bars (2 lb/in^2)

pressure and 0·03 bars (0·5 lb/in^2) vacuum, and the by-pass valve (28). An alternative to the common mast riser would be the provision of individual short stack vents to each tank. There are extensive safeguards designed to give visual and aural indications of abnormal operating conditions, and even to shut down the system if predetermined parameters are exceeded. Among these parameters are high O_2 content, failure of the scrubbing tower water supply, and low gas pressure. To ensure that the pressure and oxygen content have been adequate throughout the inerting operation, the installation of a continuous chart recorder for these criteria would be recommended.

The foregoing is a brief description of the system and a condensed version of its operation is as follows. Starting with the ship coming out of dry dock with all tanks clean and full of fresh air, by-pass valve (28) being shut, the system is put into operation and inert gas is blown into each tank in turn (22), the tank contents being vented to atmosphere through the purge pipe (25). The exhausting atmosphere is regularly monitored for O_2 content with portable equipment and the tank contents may be regarded as being satisfactorily inert when the reading is within about 1 per cent of the O_2 content of the entering inert gas (usually better than 5 per cent). The system is then shut down, the slight pressure in the tanks being under the control of the pressure/vacuum valve.

On loading cargo, by-pass valve (28) is opened and as the oil level rises, inert gas is expelled through the former. On completion of cargo loading, the ullage space now being filled with a mixture of inert gas and hydrocarbon vapour, valve (28) is closed, variations of pressure being under the control of the pressure/vacuum valve (27). During loaded passage, loss of pressure below a predetermined limit is made good by re-inerting up to the normal pressure.

On discharge, as the cargo is pumped out of a tank, inert gas at a slight pressure is pumped in to maintain the *status quo*. On completion, the empty dirty tanks are filled once more with inert gas. Any necessary water washing of tanks can be subsequently carried out in the safety of an inert atmosphere, the slight positive pressure ensuring that no air can enter the space through tank cleaning openings, etc.

It is of interest to note that a dirty oil tank filled with inert gas may still be hazardous under collision conditions if breached. This is because of the dilution of the contents with air brings the mixture within its flammable range. Intrinsic safety depends not only on an oxygen-deficient atmosphere, but also on one in which the flammable hydrocarbon vapour percentage volume has been reduced to an acceptable level. Figure 43 illustrates this point, the limits of flammability of hydrocarbon gases in air being approximately 2 to 12 per cent of the volume. However, as is evident from the graph, as the percentage of O_2 in the mixture decreases, so the limits of the flammable range draw closer together until at about 11 per cent of O_2, the mixture becomes non-flammable. If the condition of the inerted tank, on

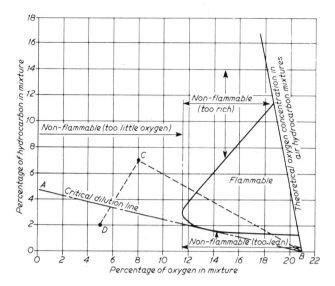

Fig. 43.—*Limits of flammability of hypothetical hydrocarbon–nitrogen/oxygen mixtures.*

being breached in collision, is given by point *C*, the subsequent dilution of the tank atmosphere with air follows the line *CB* and hence again enters the flammable zone. On the other hand, if the condition is represented by point *A*, the line *AB* does not cross the flammable zone and so the tank atmosphere on dilution never becomes explosive.

Thus, it is obvious why, after discharging cargo under inert gas, it is prudent to continue inerting until such time as the exhaust from the purge pipe shows O_2 and hydrocarbon vapour volume percentages which places the mixture below the critical dilution line.

6.7. DRY POWDER SYSTEMS

Although tankers are referred to specifically in the MS (Fire Appliances) Rules 1965, no specific reference is made to ships carrying liquid hydro-carbon gases in bulk, i.e. LNG and LPG and a moment's reflection will indicate that the types of fixed installation referred to in the Rules are not the most suitable for fighting gas fires.

Although LPG (e.g. propane and butane) may be carried in tanks under pressure at ambient temperature, they are more usually carried refrigerated whilst LNG, e.g. methane with a critical temperature of −82°C (−116°F), is always carried deeply refrigerated in the liquid state, its boiling point at ambient pressure being −162°C (−260°F).

Any leakage of such liquids from joints, valves, etc. on deck vaporizes quickly. The speed of vaporization is affected by such factors as the area over which the liquid has spread, the depth of spill, ambient temperatures,

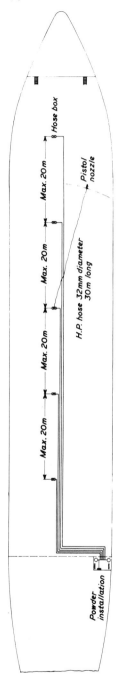

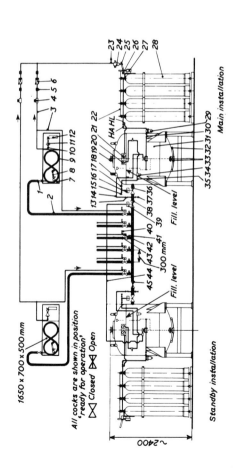

1. Stop cock.
2. Powder piping.
3. Pneumatic control piping.
4. Relief vent.
5. Siperm filter.
6. Non-return valve.
7. Hose box.
8. Pistol nozzle.
9. Powder hose.
10. Stop valve.
11. Pressure reducing valve.
12. Release cylinder (nitrogen).
13. Stop cock.
14. Flushing pipe.
15. Relief cock.
16. Pneumatic release piston.

17. Stop cock.
18. Safety valve.
19. Filling orifice.
20. Low pressure gauge.
21. High pressure gauge.
22. Release rods.
23. Relief cock.
24. Pneumatic piston.
25. Release lever.
26. Release mechanism.
27. Electric switch.
28. Pressure cylinder (nitrogen).
29. Pressure regulator.
30. Stop cock.
31. Dry chemical container.
32. Pressurizing valve.

33. Drain orifice.
34. Limit valve.
35. Pneumatic control piping.
36. Main cock dry chemical.
37. Connexion for checking and flushing.
38. Stop cock.
39. Pneumatic release piston.
40. Relief cock.
41. Flushing connexion.
42. Pneumatic release piston.
43. Direction cock.
44. Pneumatic control piping.
45. Stop cock.
HA. High pressure stop cock.
HL. High pressure feed pipe.

FIG. 44.—Diagrammatic arrangement of fixed dry chemical extinguishing installation.

etc. With the liquid temperature being so low, application of comparatively warm sea water through a fire hose, or as foam, obviously hastens its change of state from liquid to gas with all the attendant risk of explosion.

On such ships, therefore, it is preferable to provide a fixed dry powder system for use on deck to combat incipient gas fires and one such system is shown diagrammatically in Fig. 44. The arrangement consists essentially of dry powder or dry chemical in one or more vessels (31) capable of being pressurized from a bank of cylinders of N_2 (28), the former being connected to various control stations on deck; one such station or box is shown in Fig. 45. At each control station (7) there is a hose and nozzle (8 and 9), a

FIG. 45.—*Control station.*

cylinder of N_2 (12) and the appropriate controls. Referring to Fig. 44, the operation is as follows. On opening the nitrogen cylinder (12) in the control box (7), gas flows through the reducing valve (11) back to the compartment containing the dry powder installation and pneumatically opens the appropriate distribution valve (42). Simultaneously, it opens the N_2 cylinders by the action of the pneumatic piston (24), release lever (25) and release mechanism (26), the gas flowing into the dry powder container through the pressure regulator (29). The pressure in the container builds up until at about 16 bars. Then the main powder valve (36) opens automatically and the powder flows to the appropriate control box (7) via the distribution manifold, the previously opened distribution valve (42), and the piping and control cock (1). The pressure in the powder container remains constant until the few remaining kilogrammes have left the container. When the powder in the first container has been used, the second container may be brought into action by manually opening its bank of N_2 cylinders. Flow of powder back into the first container is prevented by the automatic closing of valve (38) by the pneumatic release piston (39). Flow of powder then continues as before. After use, the dry powder lines should be blown clear with compressed air or gas, the N_2 cylinders replenished and the dry powder containers refilled without delay.

The dilemma facing every master confronted with a deck fire involving LPG or LNG is, of course, whether or not to attempt to put it out. The answer to a certain extent lies in the circumstances. If, for example, a joint fails during cargo working and the issuing gas catches fire, it may well be that the fire is not involving other parts of the gas system; then, after bringing all the available fire extinguishing equipment to a state of readiness, no attempt should be made to extinguish the fire until the gas supply to the fire has been isolated. The dying fire may then be extinguished, if need be, by the use of dry powder. Adjacent fires, not involving the gas system, can be dealt with as appropriate and boundary cooling of the poop by means of jets of water from fire hoses may be prudent in the meantime to prevent the spread of fire, for example, into the accommodation.

Extinguishing a gas fire before the supply is secured, whilst being understandable, may only result in the ensuing gas–air mixture re-igniting with possible catastrophic results.

Gross spillage of deeply refrigerated liquids is dangerous in the extreme. Not only can they cause embrittlement of the deck but contact with the human body results in vicious cold burns at the very least. Whilst all fire fighting equipment should be brought to a state of readiness should such spillage occur, probably only three courses of positive action are possible:
 a) attempt to isolate the source of leakage;
 b) wash the leaked liquid overboard as quickly as possible with copious amounts of sea water from the fire hoses;
 c) extinguish or secure all possible sources of ignition until the resulting gas cloud has dissipated.
This is all far easier said than done and in case of such an emergency a prepared plan is required to be made for each individual ship, having regard to all the relevant circumstances.

6.8. STEAM SMOTHERING

Steam smothering is not a very satisfactory or efficient method of extinguishing a fire because, *inter alia*, the vapour condenses on cool surfaces and is easily dispersed by a draught. Additionally when used in cargo spaces, it damages cargo which might otherwise be salvaged. Moreover, its use can be positively dangerous in certain circumstances and in respect of explosives, the use of steam is statutorily banned.

The use of steam for the protection of cargo spaces is understandably becoming less popular and could be termed obsolescent. Although permitted by law to be used for such spaces, it is required that feed water storage or make-up arrangements be such that steam for fire fighting purposes, in addition to that required for propulsion, be continuously supplied until the end of the voyage. The dead weight and financial penalties involved in the provision of a relatively inefficient fire extinguishing system, and the conclusions to be drawn when more efficient systems are available, are therefore obvious.

In machinery spaces, steam smothering is only permitted in ships of under 1000 gross tons and even in these relatively small ships an extra 136 l (30 gal) foam fire extinguisher or equivalent is required when water tube boilers are fitted. Thus, in larger ships where the use of such boilers with their small reserve of steam capacity is widespread, the shortcomings of the protection allegedly provided is recognized and the use of steam prohibited.

6.9. VAPORIZING FLUIDS

This term covers a wide range of halogenated hydrocarbons of which we are concerned mainly with two, bromotrifluoromethane ($CBr F_3$), known as BTM or Halon 1301, and bromochlorodifluoromethane ($CBr ClF_2$), known as BCF or Halon 1211.

Although the use of BTM and BCF is accepted in principle in the U.K., no British ships have yet been so fitted, but it is only a question of time before systems utilizing these media become available and are included in the range from which the owner may make his choice.

It is considered that an ideal way to use such efficient fire extinguishing agents is to divide machinery space, where practicable, into discrete compartments where high fire risks exist, e.g. generator flats, auxiliary boiler and oil fuel separator rooms, etc. and provide each with its own separate vaporizing fluid system. Within any space, a fire which could not be readily extinguished by the appliances available would only require the space to be evacuated and closed down, and the system locally operated, all virtually instantaneously, for immediate extinction of the fire to be achieved without the need for the rest of the machinery space to be abandoned. Rapid injection of the vaporizing fluid, after detection of the fire, is essential however if the production of toxic fumes resulting from the medium coming into contact with hot metal surfaces is to be minimized.

Full scale fire tests conducted by the United States Coast Guard in 1972 on the m.v. *Rhode Island* using bromotrifluoromethane (BTM) in various concentrations resulted, *inter alia*, in the following conclusions:

    1) the medium is at least as effective as CO_2 for extinguishing large scale machinery space fires;

2) a discharge time of 10 sec or less prevents significant decomposition of the fire extinguishing medium;

3) the concentration of extinguishant decomposition products are less hazardous than the concentrations of fuel combustion products produced in the test fires.

It might be of interest to note that the Halon nomenclature for halogenated hydrocarbons is based on a five digit figure system credited to the US Army Corps of Engineers. Starting from the left, the figures denote the number of atoms of carbon, fluorine, chlorine, bromine and iodine present in the particular substance, a terminal zero being discarded. Thus, BTM ($CBr F_3$) becomes Halon 1301 and BCF ($CBr ClF_2$) becomes Halon 1211.

7. BREATHING APPARATUS

"Where there is smoke there is fire" is an old adage, and the reverse is equally true, for in an oil fire the smoke is often as difficult to contend with as the fire. Likewise, when a space is closed down to confine a fire or the air supply is restricted to stifle it, the O_2 content is quickly reduced to the point where the atmosphere would not support life. These considerations make it imperative to have some appliances available to allow the fire fighters to enter such a smoke-laden or suffocating atmosphere and to maintain their air supplies. Firemen's outfits, required to be carried on most ships, therefore include breathing apparatus the number and type depending on the class and size of vessel. Breathing apparatus may be of the smoke mask or helmet type, or of the self-contained compressed air type, though at least one of the breathing apparatus provided in any ship is required to be of the former type. The type wherein a mask (as shown in Fig. 46) is supplied with air through a flexible hose from either a bellows unit or a rotary blower, will be found in nearly every ship, whilst the self-contained type in which the wearer carries a supply of air in a high pressure cylinder on his back is often carried as well. Where an air hose exceeding 120 ft in length would be necessary to reach from the open deck well clear of any hatch or doorway to any part of the accommodation, service, cargo or machinery space, at least one breathing apparatus of the self-contained type must be carried in addition. With the particular unit shown in Fig. 47, the cylinders contain the equivalent of 1600 l of air, compressed to 138 bars (2840 lb/in^2), the minimum statutory capacity of free air being 1200 l. This is first reduced to about 6 bar (80 lb/in^2), in a reducing valve (Fig. 48) and then passes to a "demand valve" which further reduces the pressure and passes air as the wearer inhales and closes when he exhales. A means for overriding the automatic air supply is incorporated for emergencies and permits air to be supplied to the mask without going through the reducing valve; Fig. 48 illustrates such an arrangement. Other units differ in detail but all types have automatic valves which release the air from the mask as the wearer exhales. A pressure gauge is always provided along with some means to indicate audibly to the wearer when 80 per cent of the cylinder capacity has been exhausted. The air hose type is the easier of the two types with which the user can become accustomed, but is somewhat cumbersome in use; it can

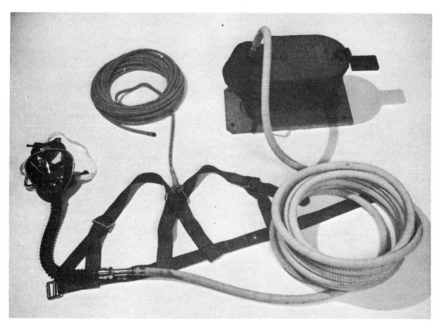

FIG. 46.—*Air line breathing apparatus.*

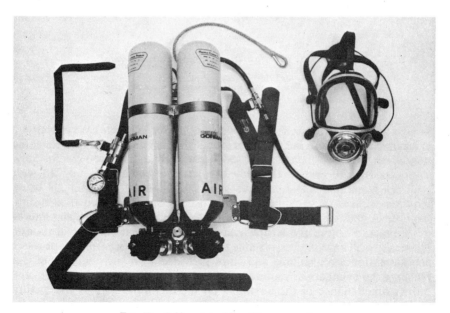

FIG. 47.—*Self-contained breathing apparatus.*

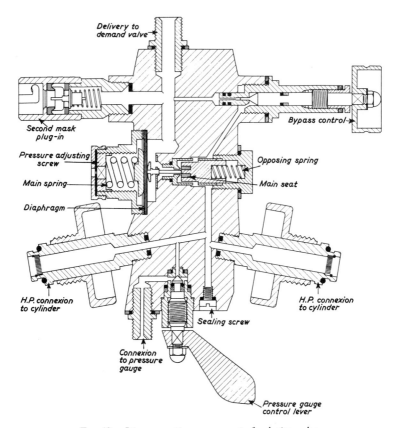

FIG. 48.—*Diagrammatic arrangement of reducing valve.*

be used as often as required, which means that everyone can have experience of wearing the outfit in fire practice; even if the air pump is stopped for some reason, the person in the mask can still breathe, though not too comfortably. In contrast, there are usually only two spare air cylinders supplied with each self-contained set—a reserve supply of at least 2400 l of air being required—and as these cylinders cannot usually be replenished aboard ship, their use in practice drills must be limited. Yet this is the type which requires more practice before the wearer can be confident and efficient in its use. However small air compressors able to deliver pure air free from oil or water contamination are available and ships provided with such equipment can recharge the cylinders as required. Regular attention should be paid to the proper maintenance of the air filters on these compressors as the quality of the air pumped into the cylinders, and hence ultimately a man's life, depends on their efficacy.

The face mask type must be adjusted to fit the face correctly before the wearer ventures into a smoke-laden atmosphere. This can be checked by nipping the supply line or stopping the supply of air at the valve and trying to breathe in, when the mask should be drawn tight in to the face and any leakage from outside is made obvious. The necessary leak-tight fit will usually not be found possible on personnel wearing beards or sideburns. It is unwise for anyone to operate in a breathing apparatus if they have recently been exposed to a smoke-laden atmosphere or suffer from respiratory trouble; and whenever possible a period of rest and deep breathing in clear air is advisable before donning a mask. If the user of one of the air hose type feels that he is not getting enough air, one tug on the lifeline will indicate to the person at the pump that more air is required; meanwhile one should not panic but remember that the air one requires can be cut down to about $\frac{1}{5}$th by relaxing and moving slowly. The correct signals for use between the person wearing the apparatus and those supporting him are printed on the box or bellows and on a label attached to the set and these signals should be strictly adhered to.

Either type of unit can be provided with a self-energized telephone system. The wire connecting the wearer with the outside world is incorporated in the lifeline which is always supplied with these sets. This telephone is very seldom fitted to the sets provided aboard ships, which is rather surprising for it would be of such inestimable value in almost all circumstances requiring the use of the breathing apparatus.

A complete "Fireman's Outfit" consists of a breathing apparatus, an axe (usually insulated), and an electric hand lamp of approved design; this lamp should give light for three hours and when supplied to tankers and bulk carriers carrying certain chemicals, it is of a "certified safe" type.

A relatively new addition in the marine field of breathing apparatus, albeit not accepted for statutory purposes, is the self-contained trolley unit. This piece of equipment was designed specially for inspection and rescue purposes because of the greatly increased depth of cargo tanks in the modern tanker. A typical unit is shown in Figs 49 and 50.

The type illustrated consists essentially of two standard compressed air cylinders, a reducing valve, pressure gauge and up to 90 m (300 ft) of high pressure air hose wound on a drum, the whole being mounted on a wheeled trolley. The free end of the air hose can be connected either into a simple face mask or into a self-contained breathing apparatus fitted with an external air connexion. In both cases, air is supplied from the trolley unit cylinders, through the reducing valve, to the face mask demand valve, the cylinder supply in the case of the self-contained breathing apparatus being shut off. The trolley unit cylinders can be changed over and replaced without interrupting the air supply, so that personnel operating far from the open air need not be dependent on the limited supply they carry. Should the need arise, in the case of personnel wearing self-contained breathing apparatus, the carried cylinder supply can be turned on and the remote supply

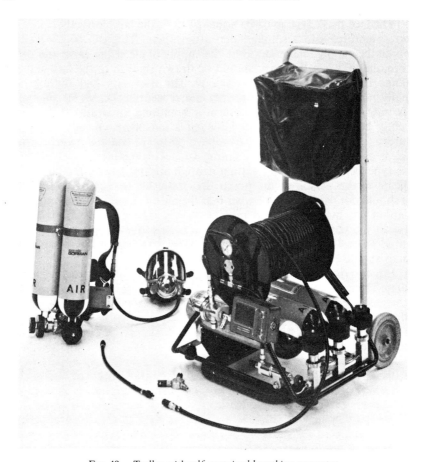

FIG. 49.—*Trolley with self-contained breathing apparatus.*

disconnected; the wearer is then dependent on his own supply and is connected to his point of entrance by his lifeline only.

A further refinement of the unit is the ability for it, in its turn, to take its air supply from the ship's compressed air main through special filters designed to eliminate oil and moisture. Alarms are built into the system and designed to operate should the ship's air supply be inadvertently shut down.

As already stated, such a unit is additional to rule requirements, but its provision affords splendid opportunities for realistic training with self-contained breathing apparatus without recourse having to be made to the limited supply of cylinder air.

It is important to remember that those men detailed to wear breathing apparatus should arrive at the scene in the best possible physical state and

FIG. 50.—*Trolley unit for self-contained breathing apparatus.*

the following drill should be observed:

   1) the wearer should walk and not run to the point at which he will put
      on the apparatus, particularly in the larger vessels where very con-
      siderable distances and heights can be involved. Other members of
      the crew should be detailed to carry all the gear and run out the
      fire fighting equipment;

2) one man should be detailed to assist the wearers of the sets;
3) test apparatus thoroughly before entering the fire area;
4) the wearer should consciously think of the "THREE C's"— *COOL, CALM* and *COLLECTED* to be in the best possible state, both physically and mentally to fight and beat any fire.

8. FIRE FIGHTING ON BOARD SHIP

8.1. BASIS OF FIREFIGHTING—*FIRE*

In order to train ourselves to do the right thing should a fire break out, we can do no better than consider the very word *FIRE* and to think of it as *F* for *FIND*, *I* for *INFORM*, *R* for *RESTRICT*, and *E* for *EXTINGUISH*.

First we must *FIND* the fire and learn what we can of its size and location. This may involve special dangers because of flammable material nearby, and these must be considered in reaching a decision as to the best course of action.

Then we must *INFORM* immediately, give the alarm and let the whole fire-fighting strength be mobilized even if the fire seems a small one. The sooner the emergency is known to those in charge the greater the chance of a rapid and successful conclusion.

R is for *RESTRICT*, to confine the fire to the smallest possible space, to see that the defences are effective and that there is no weak spot which could allow the fire to spread to another compartment.

Finally, *E* for *EXTINGUISH* to choose the most suitable extinguishers for the particular situation, and to overcome the fire as rapidly as possible.

Of course there is always the occasion when these actions are dealt with so rapidly that they do not seem to be separate items. Perhaps a flickering light is seen at the boiler front, someone shouts "Fire", grabs a foam extinguisher, tips it up and out goes the fire. A possible conflagration has been extinguished so quickly that its dangers may not have been appreciated. Many ship fires do not have such a successful outcome, for unless the cause is investigated and steps are taken to see that it cannot happen again, the fire may not be spotted so quickly next time.

Let us examine the methods of fire fighting and the appliances provided in more detail in the light of these four headings.

8.1.1. Finding the Fire

Methods of detecting a fire in the accommodation, cargo and storage spaces are incorporated in almost all passenger ships, and many cargo ships have detection systems in the cargo spaces. These are very useful but best of all is the detection system which all ships carry—the human nose. This is the most sensitive system of all, its detecting properties being so acute that in many instances the only indication of an incipient fire has been an elusive smell of smoke. Should your nose give you such a warning do not ignore it, report the occurrence and see that it is investigated or you may be sorry later.

The value of the human nose is admitted by the makers of fire detection systems using the smoke indicating cabinet, for the exhaust gas is released above the helmsman's head, and he can often smell the smoke before it can be detected at the cabinet. Unfortunately, the smells emanating from certain cargoes such as dried blood, hides, and some chemicals are such that no self-respecting helmsman could be asked to endure, so a by-pass valve is fitted to release the air outside the wheelhouse. Even so, the helmsman should sample the exhausting air at regular intervals, though being human he does not always do this. When a sprinkler system is fitted, the alarm is given automatically as has already been described, whilst even where a sprinkler system is not required under the Regulations, the alternative electrical detection system previously described may be fitted in accommodation spaces of passenger ships.

In larger passenger ships, a fire patrol makes continuous rounds of the ship, clocking in at specially placed controls to make sure that they visit every part of the ship in turn.

The detection of fires in other ships is dependent upon keen and alert watchkeeping, both on and off duty, for every ventilator, stairway, alleyway or even the louvres in cabin doors may serve to indicate an incipient fire before it has time to reach dangerous proportions.

8.1.2. Informing

Should the occasion arise the crew will be informed of a fire and of the need to organize themselves into fire parties by an agreed system of whistle blasts and alarm bells operated from the bridge. It is imperative, therefore, that the person in charge on the bridge should have an immediate notification of any fire wherever it may be by means of the telephone or direct alarm if one is fitted. Of course, if a small fire is found in the early stages and there is a portable extinguisher available it should be used, and immediate measures should be taken to confine the fire. But at the same time, any possible means should be used to give the alarm, even to shouting "Fire" to attract attention, for there is usually someone within hearing distance, particularly in the machinery spaces. Should the use of the portable extinguisher be insufficient to prevent the spread of the flames, and should it not be possible to attract attention, then a cool mind and good judgement are at a premium; one person alone must decide the right time to leave the fire in order to give the alarm. The longer that only one person knows of the emergency, then the greater is the possibility of it getting out of hand. This is no time for mock heroics because there is also the danger that one may be overcome or cut off and the position could well be hopeless before someone else discovers the blaze. Even if one is cut off, there may still be ways of attracting attention; for example, by turning the cock on a low level boiler water alarm, or a low pressure oil or water alarm, whilst the flashing of accommodation lights or even hammering on a light steel bulkhead will usually attract attention. If one must leave the scene of the fire to give the alarm, any doors or openings admitting air to the space should be closed, fans with accessible controls should be stopped. If the fire is in the boiler room, the fuel should be shut off, quick closing valves being provided at the boiler room fronts for this purpose.

8.1.3. Restricting the Fire

In one instance, a fire in an auxiliary boiler room spread to the engine room and accommodation only because the first person on the scene dropped a two gallon extinguisher in the doorway and prevented the door from closing, so that instead of a comparatively minor fire the ship was almost a total loss.

This shows the importance of taking the necessary steps possible when a fire has been found and the alarm given, so that its spread will be limited, and to ensure that the positions from which it is to be attacked will not become untenable. Each fire must be treated according to its own peculiarities, but the aim should always be the same—to restrict the fire to the compartment in which it originated, or to the smallest area around which defences can be maintained. Always remember that a fire has six sides, and it is of little use preventing the spread of the fire into the next compartments if the deck above and below are red hot and fires are breaking out in these places. There are certain natural barriers built into every ship, and these must be used to best advantage in checking the spread of the fire. In passenger ships, the accommodation will be constructed in vertical zones which are isolated from each other by fire proof bulkheads, so that should one zone be untenable, the fire can be attacked from an adjacent zone. Within these vertical zones there are alternative methods of protection. If a sprinkler system is fitted it is considered safe enough to require a lower standard for incombustible materials, but if not then all the internal bulkheads will be of fire resistant construction, often with very restricted use of combustible materials for furniture and fittings. Special arrangements are provided to prevent the vertical spread of fire via stairways and lift shafts. In older cargo ships there may be little provision for fire breaks in the accommodation, except that each block is usually in a steel deckhouse and may have some internal steel divisions. Under the Merchant Shipping (Cargo Ship Construction and Survey) Rules 1965 however, in cargo ships of 4000 gross tons and over, not only do the superstructure, structural bulkheads, decks and deckhouses have to be constructed of steel, but the corridor bulkheads, serving accommodation spaces and control stations require to be of steel or incombustible "B" class panels, slight relaxations being permitted in certain circumstances. This should help to prevent some of the serious fires which have often originated from a dropped cigarette end or a match which was not properly extinguished.

If smoke is seen coming from, or a fire is detected in a cabin the alarm should be given and when possible the finder should see that there is no one asleep there or on the floor. If the door is initially closed, care should be taken to ensure that when it is opened the air so admitted does not cause a smouldering fire to flare up. If he leaves the scene to get an extinguisher and to give the alarm, the finder should close the door and also any open portholes. This may seem an elementary precaution, yet it is amazing how often the most elementary precautions are neglected. Even a wooden door or bulkhead will restrain a fire long enough to allow proper fire appliances to be brought to bear, whereas an open door or porthole will provide the draught to spread the flames at an alarming rate.

Notwithstanding the foregoing, the whole question of structural fire protection in cargo ships is presently under active consideration by IMCO. It is expected that the eventual recommendations in this respect will provide a far higher degree of built in fire protection than hitherto obtained.

The arrangements provided in the boiler and machinery spaces to prevent the spread of fire vary greatly from one ship to another, but certain general principles apply. Boiler rooms are usually separated from the engine room by a bulkhead, and if this is water-tight it can be used to isolate the boiler room. Doors which might allow the spread of fire between such spaces should be self-closing or have means whereby they may be closed from outside the space, and such doors should never be propped or wedged open. Beware of the steel screen bulkhead which might appear fire proof, but is pierced for the passage of pipes or has a bilge common with the engine room; it will allow burning oil to flood through and start a blaze in that space. Such spaces should not be thought of as separate but should be dealt with as a whole. The machinery spaces should have steel covers to the engine room skylights and fiddley casings, steel flaps to close the ventilators and the annular spaces between the inner and outer funnel, and an extension to the control for the tunnel watertight door, all of which can be operated from outside the space concerned. External arrangements are also provided whereby all ventilating and forced draught fans can be stopped, oil pumps can be stopped, and suction valves for oil tanks above the level of the tank top can be shut.

The covers to engine room casings are often called "skylights", but in these days when all ships have a high standard of electric lighting, it seems that the ventilating effect of these openings is more important and there is little reason why they should still be made of glass, even if it is heat resisting. Windows in machinery casings, even if they are fitted with drop down steel shutters, are weaknesses in the fire defences of a ship, and are no longer fitted.

8.1.4. Extinguishing the Fire

The most important rule in fire fighting is speed of attack. The exception to this rule is that it is sometimes better to isolate a cargo hold by blanking off ventilators and relying on smothering steam or gas to keep the fire down until reaching port, meantime cooling bulkheads in adjoining spaces to ensure that the fire does not spread. In other cases, it is sometimes necessary to close the entrances to a space until more effective appliances can be brought to bear; but generally the longer the fire goes on, the less is the chance of it being easily subdued. Remember, either the fire is being subdued or it is gaining ground, in which case it must be considered whether the methods being employed are the most effective ones available, or whether it would be wise to confine the fire for a little while till dispositions have been altered to better advantage for a renewed attack. Persons fighting a fire on deck or in accommodation should keep to windward if possible; meanwhile, the ship should be manoeuvred so as to attempt to blow the flames overboard, that is, if the fire is aft the ship should be headed into the wind and if it is forward the ship should be slowed down with the wind astern. The effect of loose water in accommodation or 'tween decks must be borne in mind, for this reduces the stability of the ship, and has caused a number of ships to capsize. Thus, it is necessary to see that all the water that is used is put to good effect. The use of controllable outlet nozzles must be advantageous as a lot of water can run to waste from an open nozzle before a hose can be directed on a fire. However, the spray nozzles usually provided can be screwed down to the extent of shutting off the water altogether when not required. This makes them superior to use, particularly when cooling down hot areas after a fire for the minimum amount of water required can be used at all times. This applies also when sorties are to be made, say, down a long corridor, for with an open jet a lot of water will be uselessly released before the operator reaches the scene of the fire. In fighting accommodation fires which have gained a good hold, one must beware of the "flash over" of the fire to other combustible materials. When heated such materials give off a flammable gas and may reach the state where they will either ignite spontaneously or will flare up quickly from the smallest spark. This phenomenon is common in forest fires and often endangers the lives of the fire fighters; the only precaution is to see that all surrounding materials are well cooled by a water spray, and that any loose material is removed from harms way.

The fire most feared by land firemen is the basement fire, because of the difficulty of access due to the smoke and heat rising to every entrance. This situation is very common aboard a ship, so that if there is a possibility of getting on the same level as the fire or beneath it, then this approach is to be preferred. If smoke is dense, a breathing apparatus should be used, but anyone who is caught and cannot see or breathe should lie or kneel on the floor as the smoke is usually less dense and it is cooler lower down. This does not apply if CO_2 has been released as this falls to the bottom of a space and could suffocate anyone lying on the floor. If a fire on deck or in accommodation is accompanied by a great deal of smoke, the machinery space ventilators should be shut and the fans stopped for although it may be uncomfortable down below, it will be possible to keep the machinery and pumps going. Many a ship has had the machinery spaces evacuated because smoke from a fire elsewhere made it impossible to stay down below.

8.2. GALLEYS

Extinguishers in and around galleys should be of a type suitable for use on fires involving burning fat or oil, e.g. foam, CO_2 or dry powder. A water jet should not be used in such cases, but it sometimes happens that a person running along an alleyway, on hearing an alarm, can pick up a soda–acid extinguisher on the way, and the result may be extremely dangerous.

A blanket of incombustible material, i.e. a fire blanket, is an extremely useful first aid appliance in a galley. Its expeditious use for example, over a fire involving a cooking utensil containing oil, can rapidly reduce a dangerous fire situation to one of manageable proportions.

It is important that fat should not be allowed to accumulate in the galley flues as fires have occurred from this cause, especially where the flues pass up through a number of decks. Some companies have fitted a fixed localized CO_2 system to the flue, a commendable idea, a damper at the flue outlet having to be closed before the system is activated. Notwithstanding the fitting of such a system, however, regular action to prevent the build up of fat in the flue is important and when filters are fitted to remove the oil from the fumes, these should be cleaned or renewed at frequent intervals.

8.3. MACHINERY SPACES

Any fire in the machinery spaces should be fought systematically and all available appliances should be brought to bear as rapidly as possible. At the same time, any sources of additional oil which might assist the spread of the fire and all fans and openings which would assist the supply of air to the fire should be shut off. It might be wise at first to leave casings open on the top of the space as this will assist the dispersal of the smoke, and providing the admission of air to the space is restricted, the violent blow lamp effect created by the draught will not be experienced. If the fire has got a hold it should *not* be attacked with a 9 l (2 gal) extinguisher since that is only so much time wasted; it is better to concentrate on the use of extinguishers which are of superior calibre to the size of the fire—in other words, one should avoid "fighting a fire" and overwhelm it instead. That is why it is so important to have the fire hoses and spray nozzles already assembled, with an adequate supply of water at all times, and preferably with foam solution and a foam-making nozzle on hand. With these brought rapidly into action, very few fires would get beyond those first few critical minutes.

The machinery spaces should only be evacuated as a last resort; there is a tendency to think that once a fire has started and the use of portable or even non-portable extinguishers has proved abortive, the engine room should be evacuated and battened down to be followed by the admission of smothering gas or foam. This is a fallacy for the nerve centre of the ship should not be given up so long as the spaces are habitable, the fire pumps and other appliances are operating satisfactorily, and a means of escape is assured. It may prove much more difficult to regain the initiative and re-enter the spaces than it was to leave, for control of the main pumps and many fire fighting appliances has been surrendered and reliance must now be placed on the fixed installation and the emergency fire pump. By using two persons working as a team, it is sometimes possible to remain and fight a fire in a space which would otherwise be untenable. One uses a hose giving a fine spray which forms a protective curtain, whilst the other uses a hose giving a jet or coarser spray necessary to penetrate to the seat of the fire. This method is also very effective in gaining access to a boiler room or engine room when it is on fire, for until one has seen it in use it is difficult to appreciate how closely a fire can be approached by using the spray as a protective screen.

If foam making hoses are available they should be used to spread foam over any oil floating on tank tops, and spray can be used to cool surrounding metal parts; the steam so formed will help to reduce the updraught and a fine spray played down into the space from above may also assist in this operation. Care must be taken that the foam is evenly spread over the whole surface of the oil; sometimes there are obstructions preventing the spread of the foam, which means that some foam will have to be applied from the other side of the obstruction. If the oil is in a well, precautions should be taken to avoid flooding it over on to a larger area, thus enlarging the fire. Similarly, it occasionally happens that if the fire is in an inaccessible position the surface can be raised by flooding to a level where foam can be evenly and easily applied. The amount of water used in the machinery spaces in fighting a fire is less important from a stability aspect than in 'tween decks or accommodation; but the sinkage of the ship as a whole must be considered, especially if there are any openings or portholes near the water level or if the vessel is in harbour or shallow water. If there is a swell running, then the hull may suffer serious damage by bumping on the bottom.

The main reason for using a spray of water on burning oil fuel is that a jet of water would merely penetrate the surface, and spread or splash the burning oil around the compartment and even into adjoining compartments. If the temperature of the oil is above the boiling point of water there is the added danger that the water may sink into the oil and be turned into steam, erupting suddenly and scattering burning oil all around. This "flashing off" can be very spectacular and very dangerous to the fire fighters, being similar to the effect of throwing a cupful of water into a pan of boiling fat. The object of using water spray on a fire is to convert as much of the water into steam as possible, for the water turned to steam absorbs about six times as much heat as that which escapes as water. However, too fine a spray will not carry far enough or will be carried away from the fire by air swirls or up draught; so the spray nozzle should be adjusted to give the smallest particles consistent with them being large enough to penetrate to the heart of the fire. Care must be exercised, however, to use only the finest spray on petrol or spirit fires for the flash point of these is very low and it is unlikely that the use of water only will extinguish them. It is better to use smothering gas, foam, or powder, with a water spray to cool the surrounding materials.

If the machinery spaces must be evacuated see that all personnel are aware of this decision, then if all openings are effectively closed, fans stopped, and oil pump and settling tank valves closed, the foam or smothering gas can be admitted and if the bulkheads and other closures remain intact, the fire will go out. This seems a very definite statement, but even without any smothering gas or foam the fire would still go out if the supply of air were entirely stopped. When the O_2 content is reduced to below 15 per cent most substances will cease to burn, and even the largest engine and boiler room spaces only hold enough air to burn about $\frac{1}{2}$ ton of oil before the O_2 content would be so reduced. It is necessary, therefore, to concentrate on restricting the fire to the spaces by cooling the boundary bulkheads and to avoid supplying any air to the fire. Unfortunately, even a small explosion will often blow off the casings or burst light bulkheads and re-admit the air so necessary to combustion. Providing the closing appliances remain intact, the next problem is how and when to re-enter the spaces when it is established that the fire is out. It must be borne in mind that if any parts are hot when air is admitted then re-ignition will take place and the fire will blaze up as strongly as before, so plenty of time must be allowed to ensure that the residual heat has had time to disperse. This time may be usefully employed in ensuring that all those taking part in the operation know their particular jobs, that all necessary fire appliances have been mustered and that a suitable means of communication exists.

The best place for re-entry is from the tunnel, if there is one, for any opening made in the upper part of the space would be assailed with a blast of hot air such that any person trying to enter in that way would probably be rendered unconscious. This means that hoses with spray nozzles will have to be laid out to the tunnel door and checked for adequate water supply, probably from the emergency pump, and that breathing apparatus will require to be worn by the persons entering the space for the purpose of cooling down the hot areas. They should be engineers who have had previous experience of operating in breathing apparatus, for they must be well acquainted with the layout of the engine room. It will be necessary for someone to stand by the watertight door control and to have a signalling system arranged so that he knows when to open and close the door. It seems surprising that so little is done to render such a difficult operation easier.

The provision of a hydrant point just inside the tunnel, as is required on certain classes of ship, would avoid the trouble of leading hose from deck, down the tunnel escape and along the tunnel, whilst a light screen door just inside the tunnel at the engine room end would obviate the difficulty of man-handling the heavy water-tight door at a position remote from the scene of action. This light steel door, fitted with a hose hole and shuttered visor, could be incorporated with the water-tight door to close the aperture on the tunnel side whereas the actual water-tight door closes the aperture at the engine room side. These provisions would appear to be a worth while addition to the usual fire fighting arrangements at small extra cost and yet such arrangements are seldom if ever fitted. When the tunnel door is opened, a blast of hot gas may blow back into the tunnel, so the casing ventilators should be opened a little way to establish some circulation from the tunnel into the engine room, but this must be restricted to the minimum amount necessary because of the extra oxygen which is being allowed into the space. The first aim on re-entry is to cool everything down with a fine water spray, and to reduce the amount of smoke, so that as the atmosphere gradually returns to normal there will be no re-ignition and other personnel will be able to enter the space with extra appliances and sprayers as soon as possible. A small but important point is that, in machinery spaces where there are many obstructions, it is wise for the person wearing a breathing apparatus to pay out the air hose and/or lifeline himself, and to have some slack around his arm, otherwise one turn around an obstruction and the line may snag and he will be unable to go any further. Once the space has been re-entered and brought back to normal atmospheric conditions, services should be restored, and the bilges cleared of oil and water, and any oily surfaces hosed down and thoroughly cleaned.

8.4. Fires Involving Electrical Appliances

The usual soda–acid and foam extinguishers produce a jet of fluid which is an electrical conductor, as is sea water, so these should not be used when live electrical equipment is in or near the direct line of projection. Under these circumstances, a dry powder, CO_2, BCF or BTM extinguisher should be used, and although a fresh water type of extinguisher may be used, preferably from a distance of more than 2 m (6 ft), it is considered wiser not to use a water type of extinguisher on such a fire. Better still, isolate the section involved so that there is no electrical hazard. When the fire has been extinguished, any electrical appliance which has been wetted with salt water should be thoroughly cleaned and dried out before being put into service.

8.5. Training: Maintenance and Use of Extinguishers

These then are the fire fighting techniques and extinguishers that a Marine Engineer may have to rely on, but as every ship is an individual entity it is imperative that he should find out which extinguishers are available on each ship, where they are positioned, and how they can be applied to the best advantage. Every ship over 500 gross tons must display a Safety Equipment Certificate, a record of the equipment available being issued with this Certificate, and in addition a plan showing their disposition has to be displayed in the accommodation.

Some companies issue a booklet to all officers on joining the ship showing the disposition of the fire appliances available. This is a good idea, but such a booklet is not likely to be immediately available in an emergency.

No matter how well a ship may be equipped, the appliances will all be useless unless properly maintained and unless the personnel know how to operate them. It would be criminal to send a soldier into the firing line without ever having fired a rifle, and it is folly to expect that a Marine Engineer can fight a fire successfully without knowing how the appliances operate and how to use them to best advantage. There is a technique in using even a 9 l (2 gal) extinguisher to best effect; by using a sweeping and encircling action to reduce the area of the flames and, so to speak, sweeping the fire into a corner before finally extinguishing it. To see a beginner trying to direct a jet of foam on the desired spot with little success may be funny, but it is no joke when there is actually a fire to extinguish. Every seafarer should see that he has the necessary experience in the use of the extinguishers during fire drills, see them recharged according to the instructions and with the correct solutions at least every year, and when the time comes he will be confident in their use. These fire drills are often treated as a joke to be avoided if at all possible, or as something to watch whilst others perform, but if properly organized and entered into in the right spirit they are the best possible guarantee that a well trained fire fighting team will be available when the occasion arises. Extinguishers should be used, remote controls for fans, oil pumps and tanks operated, and every effort made to imagine the various places where fire might break out, and by actually dealing with the emergency in the conditions which would be experienced in a real outbreak, every one concerned will be competent if a fire is experienced. It is usual in fire drills to see a deck apprentice walking up and down the foredeck wearing a breathing apparatus and telling the person working the blower whether he wants more air or less. This is poor practice for operating in a smoke-laden atmosphere; better for him to be blindfolded and to find his way around a hatch, over an obstacle course, or, through various rooms in the accommodation giving the recognized signals by lifeline. Actually, the deck apprentices would be of little use in operations involving smoke-laden atmospheres in the machinery spaces where precise local knowledge is of utmost importance, yet how seldom do we find that the engineers have any experience of operating in a breathing apparatus. It is not much use trying to learn this in actual fire conditions when a mistake may mean a life, and yet confidence can only be obtained by previous experience. So everyone should join in the fire drills with the intention of learning all that can be learned from them and they should be as realistic as possible. The emergency pump should be started and seen to give an adequate supply of water at the required pressure, the fire hoses and spray nozzles used, and turns taken using the breathing apparatus so that no one will be a "passenger" if the real thing comes along. The Merchant Shipping Notice M320 obtainable from any Mercantile Marine Office gives excellent advice on how to have effective boat and fire drills.

After a fire drill, and at regular intervals, the condition of the appliances should be checked to ensure that they will be effective should they be required. Hoses, especially canvas ones must be thoroughly dried after use or mildew will attack them and when required they will be full of holes. To dry a hose properly after sea water has been used, it should be flushed through with fresh water, drained and dried thoroughly internally, preferably by passing a current of warm air through it. New lengths of hose should be uncoiled and stored more loosely, because the coils are too tight as supplied and will soon crack along the seams if left as supplied. Fire hose should not be stored in too warm a place, a temperature of under 38°C (100°F) being advisable.

Samples of foam-making solutions should be taken from the larger extinguishers at intervals and mixed in the correct proportions to see that they will still produce the required volume of foam. When a foam making system has been tested or after use the pipes and containers should be flushed with fresh water as stated previously.

Steam smothering is now usually found only in older ships in lieu of more efficient extinguishing media, but if this system is fitted then the distribution pipes should be checked whenever the holds are empty to see that they are not choked with rust and that the valve spindles are free. If blanks are fitted in the lines to holds, check that they will be accessible if there should be a fire; the bolts should be of brass and easily freed, so that the blanks can be easily removed.

Finally, the hose connexions should be clean and undamaged. It is important to regularly connect all the instantaneous couplings on board to see that these join satisfactorily. Faults to look for are:
1) build up of verdigris preventing the male and female couplings from connecting properly;
2) too heavy grease which prevents proper connexion being made;
3) rubber washers in the female couplings being too thick thus making connexion difficult;
4) the small spring-loaded locking pawls, (snugs) should be seen to be free because these tend to seize up if not attended to;
5) the seizing wire connecting couplings to hose is in good condition.

Dual purpose nozzles should be freely adjustable between jet and spray settings.

The ship-to-shore coupling adapter should be readily available so that should a fire occur in port, the Fire Brigade, who should be called immediately, will be able to supply water to the ship's fire main from the shore.

Regular maintenance is of greatest importance in keeping the equipment in a state of readiness, for even the best systems are useless if poor maintenance has rendered some vital part inoperative.

The two yearly surveys for the issue of Safety Equipment Certificate are of great assistance in this respect, but it is surprising how quickly good appliances can be rendered useless if left to look after themselves. In the early days of Safety Equipment Certificates, ships were inspected in which practically all the fire appliances were inoperative to the extent that the crew would have been helpless in the face of fire. All too often steam smothering pipes and fire main water pipes burst when water pressure was applied, valves were seized so that the spindles broke when attempts were made to open them; hand wheels and name plates were missing and no one knew which valve served which space; lines were blanked off, often with bolts which had to be sawn apart; hoses were perished and often had fittings which would not fit the hydrants; ventilator and skylight closing gear was non-existent or jammed solidly; extended spindles to pumps, fans and oil tanks were inoperative or disconnected, water pumps were unable to maintain a satisfactory pressure, emergency pumps would not start; foam systems would not make foam, portable extinguishers were often empty, wrongly filled or failed the pressure test; CO_2 storage bottles were often empty whilst breathing apparatus and loose equipment were broken or lost.

The position is usually much better now, but there is still room for improvement and many of the above faults can still be found, because there is still a widespread apathy among the Engineer Officers concerning the use and upkeep of fire appliances.

9. FIRE APPLIANCES QUESTIONS IN DEPARTMENT OF TRADE EXAMINATIONS

The requirements under the Merchant Shipping Act of 1894 that certain vessels shall carry a given complement of certificated engineers are enforced with a view to ensuring the safety of life at sea, and are embodied in the "Regulations for the Examination of Engineers in the Merchant Navy". It is not surprising, therefore, that knowledge of fire precautions, and of the principles, operation and maintenance of fire appliances together with fire detection and methods of dealing with fires play a large part in the examinations. Descriptive questions are set in the Engineering Knowledge and Naval Architecture papers and the subject is thoroughly covered in the Oral Examination, so that unless the questions are answered in a satisfactory manner, the examiner will be unable to issue a Certificate. Questions are phrased to ensure, so far as is possible, that certificated engineers will know the precautions to take to avoid conditions which might give rise to a fire, which appliances are likely to be available, which extinguishers to use under given conditions, how to maintain them in good working order so as to be immediately available, and how to apply them to best advantage.

No matter how much a Marine Engineer knows of the inner workings of fire appliances he is of little use in actually fighting a fire unless he has some experience of the operation of the appliances, and knows what kinds of fire they can be expected to subdue. It seems obvious, therefore, that as the proper use and maintenance of fire appliances is so dependent on the person responsible having had practical experience and preferably tuition in their use and maintenance that the satisfactory completion of a suitable training course is a necessary safeguard for all Marine Engineers. Practical fire fighting courses are arranged by some shipping companies and excellent courses which provide comprehensive coverage of the subject are provided by the Naval Authorities at Portsmouth and by the Merchant Navy Training Board at Leith, Plymouth, Southampton, Hull and Liverpool. In fact, such knowledge is so desirable that evidence of attendance at an approved four day course providing practical experience of fire fighting and fire appliances is now required before an Engineer Officer can be examined for a Certificate of Competency.

BIBLIOGRAPHY

The following publications are worthy of further study.

Rushbrook, F. 1961. "Fire Aboard", Technical Press, London.

Symposium papers, 1956. "Fires in Ships". *Trans. I. Mar. E.* vol. 68, pp. 471–537.

Keenan, G. L. 1955. "Fire Appliances". *Trans. I. Mar. E.* vol. 67, pp. 209–222.

Burgoyne, J. H. "Accidental Ignition and Explosions of Gases in Ships". *Trans. I. Mar. E.* vol. 77, pp. 129–141.

Nash, P. and Ashton, L. A. 1965. "Research in Fire Fighting and Fire Protection in Ships". *Trans. I. Mar. E.* vol. 77, pp. 227–251.

Murray Smith, D. R. and Willens, A. T. "Fire Protection and Fire Fighting in Ships". *Trans. I. Mar. E.* vol. 78, pp. 81–102.

Day, C. F., Platt, E. H. W., Telfer, I. E. and Tetreau, R. P. "The Development and Operation of an Inert Gas System for Oil Tankers". *Trans. RINA* vol. 114, pp. 33–72.

U.S. Coast Guard. 1972. "An Investigation into the Effectiveness of Halon 1301 (Bromotrifluoromethane) as an Extinguishing Agent for Shipboard Machinery Space Fires". Washington.

Manual of Seamanship. 1944. Part 7, "Fireboats and Ship Fires", HMSO, London.

Department of Trade and Industry. Merchant Shipping Notices:

1960. "Muster and Drills in Sea-going Ships". M320.

1967. "Fire Prevention and Fire Fighting in Ships in Port". M393.

1966. "Prevention of Fire in Cargo Ships Using Oil Fuel". M439.

1968. "Prevention of Fires during Welding Operations". M268.

1968. "Fire Fighting Arrangements in Ships Carrying Explosives". M527.

1970. "Fire Fighting on Small Cargo Ships". M591.

1972. "Fires Involving Lubricating Oil". M651.

1972. "Fire Fighting Training". M643.

Department of Trade and Industry. 1974. Survey of Fire Appliances. Instructions for Guidance of Surveyors. HMSO.